Lois — I hope you enjoy this'

Praise for *The Tell-Tale Entrepreneur*

"Storytelling is the most powerful way to engage customers. Bernard brings this point home in a relevant way to an entrepreneurial audience."

—**Mike Gianfagna, principal, Gforce Marketing, Inc.**

"I've worked with Bernard on many occasions. He's an excellent storyteller, able to blend technology, cultural references, and humor in a fascinating way."

—**Moshe Sheier, VP of marketing, CEVA, Inc.**

"When you want to plug your product, you can just serve up the facts. Not very exciting. Or you can serve up a story that will get your readers excited, jumping to your website, wanting to learn more. I've worked with Bernard for a while. He writes the second kind of story—without fail."

—**Kurt Shuler, VP of marketing, Arteris IP**

THE TELL-TALE ENTREPRENEUR

BERNARD MURPHY

The
Tell-Tale
ENTREPRENEUR

A GUIDE TO
storytelling in business

Advantage®

Published by Advantage, Charleston, South Carolina.
Member of Advantage Media Group.

ADVANTAGE is a registered trademark, and the Advantage colophon is a trademark of Advantage Media Group, Inc.

Printed in the United States of America.

10 9 8 7 6 5 4 3 2 1

ISBN: 978-1-64225-155-5
LCCN: 2020920386

Book design by Megan Elger.

This publication is designed to provide accurate and authoritative information in regard to the subject matter covered. It is sold with the understanding that the publisher is not engaged in rendering legal, accounting, or other professional services. If legal advice or other expert assistance is required, the services of a competent professional person should be sought.

Advantage Media Group is proud to be a part of the Tree Neutral® program. Tree Neutral offsets the number of trees consumed in the production and printing of this book by taking proactive steps such as planting trees in direct proportion to the number of trees used to print books. To learn more about Tree Neutral, please visit **www.treeneutral.com**.

Advantage Media Group is a publisher of business, self-improvement, and professional development books and online learning. We help entrepreneurs, business leaders, and professionals share their Stories, Passion, and Knowledge to help others Learn & Grow. Do you have a manuscript or book idea that you would like us to consider for publishing? Please visit **advantagefamily.com** or call **1.866.775.1696**.

For Laura, my favorite entrepreneur.

CONTENTS

"The most powerful person in the world is the storyteller. The storyteller sets the vision, values, and agenda of an entire generation that is to come."

—STEVE JOBS

FOREWORD

Throughout my career, and today as an investor and board member for a number of companies, I've heard a lot of presentations. I have to tell you that many of them are dreadful. Absolutely dreadful. I'm not talking about the people or the technology. And I'm definitely not talking about their PowerPoints. I'm talking about their inability to deliver a compelling story, because that's what they should be doing—telling a story—not giving a PowerPoint presentation!

What is clear as day, every time, is that when these folks begin to put the presentation together, they fire up PowerPoint, then start cranking out slides: a product slide, a technology slide, an architecture slide, a module slide, a physics slide, a programming slide, something on the market and the competitors, something about how great their opportunity is. They kick it around, remember some other stuff they should jam in there, and pretty soon they've got forty or fifty slides.

Then they start trying to optimize it—reordering, adding agenda slides so you know where they are in the pitch, putting in oh-so-clever graphics and transitions, reducing font sizes so the text fits into fewer slides, then reducing them again. Inevitably they get to the point that the people in the back of the room have no hope of reading the slides.

Now they're in trouble! They'll have twenty minutes to deliver twenty or thirty slides that are chock-full of data and text. Slides that are very clever. Slides that are very complex. When they deliver the pitch, they'll have to talk fast! They'll have to skip over a lot of what's mentioned on the slides. They'll deliver a key point, a somewhat important point, and an irrelevant point in quick succession, often in the same sentence. They won't be able to pause for emphasis, certainly not to rephrase a point or interject a specific example when they notice a quizzical look from their audience—they won't have time. The audience will have no way to know what the really key points are. If they get a few questions, the presentation runs late. They'll talk faster and faster. They'll skip over more and more. At the end they're talking at warp speed. The audience is lost. Finally, the last slide. Ah, a sigh of relief. It's over.

What a disaster! What a mess! That isn't a story, it's a data dump. Why would I or anyone else be excited about this? Where do you engage your audience? Talk about what they need? Why they should care? But this is exactly what the typical presenter does, because they think that's how it's supposed to be done.

My view—turn off your computer. Go to a conference room with a pad of 3M notes. Ask yourself: what's the story that I'm trying to tell? How can I break it up into pieces that can easily be told and understood? What are the key points that I'm trying to make? Come up with little ideas, substories. Write each on a note and stick it on the whiteboard. Build the elements of a complete story through these sticky notes. Arrange them so that the big-picture story flows naturally.

Now you can build a PowerPoint—which, by the way, should not be a straight transcription of your notes. My preference is that the PowerPoints be mostly pictures. The presentation will be the story that goes along with the picture. The right pictures will enhance the story for the audience far better than pages of bullet points. The right pictures will remind you to tell a story that you can tell naturally— you won't have to read it or memorize it!

Bernard gets it. He understands that the best presentations aren't presentations at all—they're stories as told by a storyteller. Bernard shows you how to tell a story. This book has several good examples of stories to inspire your story creation, including one of mine. It's an easy read and provides a lot of useful advice consistent with what I've just said. I think when you've finished the book, you'll have a very different view of what makes a story. If you put it into practice, you'll find that your stories will attract much more enthusiastic audiences and will convert more listeners to buyers or investors.

John East
Saratoga, California

INTRODUCTION

As far back as we care to go in our history, we've been telling stories and listening to them with wide-eyed excitement. From the earliest cave paintings to the siege of Troy, Romeo and Juliet's ill-fated love, and more recent epics—*Star Wars, Raiders of the Lost Ark, The Matrix, The Hunger Games,* and countless others—we're endlessly captivated by stories. Unfortunately, somewhere along the line, we put stories in a box marked "entertainment." In other aspects of our lives and careers—when communicating in technical, legal, or business contexts—we've become accustomed to information-heavy, excitement-free lectures, presentations, and documents. Where efficiency and accuracy are paramount, somehow storytelling seems too informal and imprecise for weighty business demands. However, efficiency is not what we need when we have to influence emotions—anticipation, fear, excitement, and trust. Then we have to turn back to stories, the programming we've developed and polished for that purpose ever since those early cave paintings. Because we respond to stories instinctively and emotionally, in a way that charts, graphs, and technical updates cannot deliver.

You may wonder, "Who cares about emotions? We're promoting/supporting our technical widget!" Take a look through the eyes of your audience. They're asking themselves, "I wonder if these people understand our needs—or are they just pushing their product at anyone they can trick into a meeting?" With a little luck, that might evolve into, "Well, it seems like they're a good fit, but do we really trust them?" Later still, you might find you have to defend your organization: "Why did we ever agree to work with these turkeys?" You know—those times when technical details are not your listeners' primary concern.

These are the most critical stages in your communications with clients, business partners, investors, your market, and ultimately, perhaps, buyers for your company—when you either surge ahead or fall out of contention. When what they care about is whether you see the world the same way they do, whether they have confidence in you, or whether they believe you are able to rebuild their broken confidence. Personal, emotionally driven decisions. Because even when we're doing serious work with serious people, we're communicating with humans, not machines.

Our primal storytelling skill has taken modern marketing by storm for just this reason. Marketing gurus have rediscovered that storytelling isn't just for entertainment. It is and always has been one of the most powerful ways we can communicate and influence. We see countless examples in consumer marketing, most often vignettes rather than full stories—images of cars sweeping along Highway 1 in Big Sur; families enjoying happy times because they use the right dishwashing soap, cereal, or home security system. That kind of "brand story" has become ubiquitous in the marketing world. In this book, however, I'm going to be talking about storytelling for communicating to businesses, where complete stories in one form or another are even more important. Take selling, where we know—and our clients, investors, prospects, and buyers know—that the road from a typical vision to execution is often bumpy and may even drop off a cliff. Those partners and potential partners want you to want to talk about real applications, with problems, and how you overcame those problems. The real story.

You might be thinking, "Oh, I completely agree! I always try to tell a story in my PowerPoint presentations!" Good for you, but what you're building may not be a story. A PowerPoint isn't a story. Nor is a white paper, or a blog, or a YouTube video. Those are delivery platforms. The story is something independent of delivery. It's the heart of what you want to communicate, equally at home in an elevator pitch, a slide-free talk, or any other medium. Once you have a story, you can tell it using any medium you choose.

One more point. You might be convinced that you don't need any help. The brilliance of your product and your innate marketing talents are enough. Good for you. But if you're like me, you enjoy studying other successful people and learning from how they have faced both trials and triumphs. I think you'll find many useful insights embedded in the real-life business stories that I'm going to share. Just for grins, I encourage you to do a little Googling for *good product bad marketing.* Check out a sampling of high-profile bombs like the Apple Newton, Microsoft Zune, or VW Phaeton. They're the tip of the iceberg. Underwater are tens, maybe hundreds of thousands of ventures with fantastic products undermined by poor marketing. Ventures that sank without a trace. You probably know a few. Maybe they were defeated by a conspiracy. Maybe by leaders or customers who didn't get it. Or maybe they just didn't tell their story very well.

HOW TO USE THIS BOOK

The goal of this book is to help you find inspiration to write your own story, not to spell out a recipe. You are smart and imaginative (why else would you be an entrepreneur?), and you already know the bones of your story. You just need a little nudge to bring out the excitement in it.

Each chapter in this book is built around a story. They're all true stories, decorated with a little creative license on my part to add more interest to the flow. After a couple of chapters in which we'll examine the elements of a story, we'll follow a path that leads through stories of tech startups, the journey from startup to investment, growing pains for established companies, and finally to an exit. I've even added a personal bonus story at the end.

I recommend you look at each as an example of the complete story you might tell your internal team or an especially nervous customer. Build this first. You might use 3M notes on a whiteboard. I prefer MS Word, developing the story as a written story without the awkward constraints of slide presentation software. Choose whatever medium best suits your taste, as long as it doesn't force you into bad habits. Don't start in PowerPoint. Slides can provide a helpful backdrop for illustrating a story, but they're a very misleading medium for developing one.

Once you have that story, you can use different pieces in different contexts. You can use the beginning to set up a real customer application. You can build on challenges you've seen along a bumpy path to show your experience in navigating those real-life problems.

Naturally, you will want to use the happy ending to show you really have delivered—you've made others successful.

Finally, this book is based on a very small sample of stories. For example, my exit story is about just one M&A exit—no IPOs, no private equity, no other M&As. For inspiration, you don't need a catalog of possibilities. You just need a few hints and examples and your own imagination.

ABOUT ME

I've been fortunate and more than a little lucky to work for most of my career in Silicon Valley, in and around the semiconductor industry. For almost forty years, I have built and sold products to household names and names behind those names in our modern electronic and computerized world. I've sold to Apple, Samsung, Intel, Cisco, Ericsson, Qualcomm, NVIDIA and many other companies, supporting the technologies they build for your cell phone, fitness watch, GoPro, Wi-Fi, and cell stations. I've also sold to the companies that support the mega-data centers behind Amazon, Google, Facebook, Baidu, Tencent, and Alibaba, and I've sold to the companies that support the explosion of automation in modern cars, our smart homes, smart buildings, and smart cities.

Over nearly forty years in the industry, I graduated up the corporate hierarchy, across multiple companies, from software developer to CTO. I've seen every side of a venture, from hands-on engineering, to applications and sales, to marketing, and from management to the executive level. And I've represented those companies to customers in conferences, webinars, panels, and blogs. I have a pretty rounded view of business communications, at its best and at its worst.

Toward the end of my "official" career, I started to write, mostly blogging for trade journals. After developing countless product-related documents over the years, I was fortunate (again) to be given significant freedom to speculate about technology and industry futures. When my company was acquired, I finally had the time to leverage that curiosity and turn it into a blogging gig. Readers noticed and companies started to request my help to boost their content marketing. That grew further into requests for assistance with messaging, as well as into executive and board roles and a couple of books for clients. Gratifying to have the time and means to share my experience with others? Absolutely.

Throughout this period, I've been further polishing my storytelling skills, and judging by the positive feedback I heard, I've started to realize just how big the need is in the worlds of technology, science, and engineering for writing that transcends the technical. Practical, left-brain professionals are not often fluent in the subtle art of connecting with other people instinctively or emotionally. More and more, I'm asked to be the go-to person for big-picture projects like corporate vision statements, or simply to help executives improve their writing—not writing typical red-line reviews, but inspiring staff and adding passion and clarity of message in selling ideas.

Which made me think about a legacy—I should share these lessons, write a book.

My first thought, my Plan A, was a book titled (I kid you not) *How Not to Suck at Technical Writing*. All of my fellow techies are clever, even brilliant in much of what they do. But there's one almost invariable exception. They cannot write to save their lives. This book would help them write more effectively.

There was a flaw in that plan. Those brilliant people not only can't write well but also can't communicate with anyone who isn't a brilliant expert in the same field. Many have no idea how what they do will affect the man or woman in the street, enterprise, boardroom, or anywhere else outside their narrow domain. That's OK when you're writing conference papers or talking to a customer almost as knowledgeable as you are, but it's no help when you're talking to people who make budget decisions—people with more of an eye on business implications than technical details.

Which is a shame, because we all had the same storytelling programming wired into our DNA tens of thousands of years ago. What these techies lack is not the native ability to tell stories. They need to discover that ability, give themselves permission to use it, and get more practice directing that skill to the right ends.

OK, Plan B. I should teach science, engineering, and technology professionals how to draw out their natural storytelling ability. Teach them how to start by explaining how what they're promoting is important to the needs of their customers, in terms relevant to the larger needs of those customers, rather than launching right into a cold, technical explanation. Also, I should expand my audience to include product marketing and applications people, because they just as often struggle to engage their audience, build interest, and get across the big picture. But then the businessman in me surfaced, and I started to worry about scalability. Does this mean that every presentation and white paper needs a variant for every different customer and every different need? With the help of my writing coach, I finally understood what was wrong with Plan B.

First, I was confusing the medium with the message.[1] My goal is to help you, my audience, build your message as effectively as you can. The content, not the delivery, which (as I said earlier) is a separate consideration. Second, I want to help you develop the message in the

---

1   With apologies to Marshall McLuhan.

form of a story, for all the reasons I've outlined.

* * *

Finally, I had my Plan C: *Storytelling for Entrepreneurs*. I settled on that plan, and this is that book. I hope you enjoy it, and I hope you find inspiration in these stories![2]

---

2   I refined the title later.

CHAPTER 1

An Accidental Story

I have convinced myself I cannot tell jokes. I arrived at this conclusion through years of trying to tell jokes and having them fall flat. At college, I tried a shaggy dog story, embellishing with lots and lots of detail, as you should in such stories. A good friend, Terry, was in the room, doubling over in laughter. Laying it on a bit thick, I thought—I couldn't be telling it that well. As I got near the end, I realized I'd forgotten to mention the central point of the story, the only thing that made it funny. Terry, at this point, was almost choking. My best friend not only hadn't warned me; he was nearly delirious at the prospect of my inevitable humiliation. For some reason, Terry remained a good friend, but I decided to stop telling jokes. Which is a shame, because if I had practiced more, I would have improved.

Jokes are nothing more than short stories, with a twist and timing. Regular stories are more forgiving, and they're much more powerful. A joke makes your listeners laugh. A story can change their minds. Storytelling is how you can convince a business partner, prospect, or investor that you are exactly who they have been looking for; that you are their best option to help them further their goals. Stories engage their imagination and their emotions—excitement, anticipation, and trust. You might think we're all supremely logical, but emotions convert skeptics into believers. Facts do not. You need to learn how to tell stories.

Emotions convert skeptics into believers. Facts do not. You need to learn how to tell stories.

We all have the storytelling gene. We don't recognize it because we're almost always listeners, not tellers. All that separates those storytellers from us is an understanding of the basic principles, reinforced by practice. You can't be a good joke-teller, a good piano player, or a good golfer unless you learn a little and practice what you've learned. The same applies to storytelling.

Don't panic. I'm not suggesting that you have to devote months or years before you can tell good stories. Without doubt, the more stories you tell, the more you'll improve. But the most important step in storytelling is inspiration—recognizing stories among the rich vein of business adventures you and your colleagues have already lived. You're surrounded by stories. You just need a little extra help to shape and deliver them effectively. I'm going to show you how to do that in the best way I know—by telling you stories.

I want to begin with a personal story, one I'll never forget. I had to give a crucial presentation to an angry Japanese customer. My team and I had prepared a top-notch pitch backed up by a slick slide deck. What we didn't understand at the time was that we needed to communicate with the customer rather than present at them. When it came my turn to present, instead I told a story—by accident. Storytelling wasn't a skill I had practiced. I'm not sure I was even aware that I was telling a story. In spite of my inexperience, it was after that meeting in Osaka that I first realized the power of storytelling in business.

* * *

Back in 1989, after nearly a decade in engineering, I joined the sales team of a large software company as a partner manager for several major accounts. One of those accounts was Mitsubishi, and I was jazzed. High-profile account, lots of in-house attention, travel to Japan. Still, I had to build on my strengths, so I dug into Mitsubishi's technical expectations.

That turned out to be not so pretty. We had been promising a lot, a major rework, integrating products, making them easier and more efficient to use. Our vision was great, our execution not so much. Going through slides and notes from earlier partnership reviews and talking with the account team, it was pretty obvious we had a track record of overpromising and underdelivering.

I wasn't worried. Without problems to solve, how could I make my mark? This was perfect, better than perfect. I joined meetings with the product teams. We debated the major goals and subgoals, what we thought we needed to work on next, and what could be pushed out. Someone suggested I join the weekly Research and Development (R&D) prioritization meetings, and I jumped at that too.

Prioritization meetings are how R&D decides which of the hundreds or thousands of requested fixes and enhancements will be allowed into the next release of the software. We would huddle around a table in a small cramped room, arguing over long and detailed lists of open issues, trying to decide what would and would not make the cut. The engineers didn't seem to mind my being involved in this process; I was one of them and understood at least some of the complexities of each issue. I also respected that I couldn't have all the fixes I wanted. I, too, had to prioritize.

Of course, as the in-house voice of Mitsubishi, one of our most important customers, I had an edge. This account commanded attention and support. I was in charge of ensuring that they were happy with our work. Everyone knew this, and the organization lined up right behind me. I loved it.

As the next partner review approached, I knew that I would have to prepare an update for the Mitsubishi team. Like most of us, my brain switched to PowerPoint. What were the slides I needed to present? They should be positive. Someone else at the meeting would take care of apologies for the delay. My job was to show we were making solid progress.

> *I made an assumption here. Someone else would fall on their sword; that would satisfy Mitsubishi, and I could get on with explaining my update. The update would parade all the wonderful work I had been doing, casting me as the hero riding in to rescue everyone. Bad idea, as I learned later.*

I went back to the program commitments and slides from the last review and picked out the main deliverables expected from my team. They didn't look so bad, given the progress we had been making. I could set green check marks (done) against a bunch of commitments. I split the progress items across a few slides so I could emphasize all the good stuff that was already underway for the next release. To further reinforce the positive message, I followed each of these slides with a summary of technical advantages gained by completing those steps—how much Mitsubishi would already be able to do with what we had completed, underlining the great progress we were making on their behalf.

Now for the difficult part, the commitments we wouldn't be able to complete for the next release. I had to find a positive spin for each. For some, it was clear we needed more discussion before we could complete a sensible implementation. I listed the points on which we needed further clarification. Once resolved, we could roll these into a following release.

Some others had proven to be more complex than we expected. I listed why these were complex, what we were doing to address that complexity, and by when we thought we could have solutions implemented. I played up the importance of making sure our implementation was correct, not just rushing out a quick fix. As for the remaining items, they had fallen victim to prioritization. We simply couldn't tackle all those fixes within the next planned release. I made a list and was careful to double-check that none of them was very important.

I was feeling pretty pleased with myself. I'd put a lot of work into planning the progress of the meeting in my slides, carefully managing how my customer would react at every step. The background illustrations, charts, and copy were some of my best. I was going to be in complete control. I was ready.

The meeting was going to be held at the Itami Dai Ichi works in southwestern Japan. For me, this was also exciting. I'd never visited Japan before—great food, history, and architecture, and maybe I could even learn a little of the language. I couldn't wait.

Just before we left, we had an all-hands account team review. Jan, the Japan country manager, dialed in. He told us he had a call the previous day with the Mitsubishi manager, who I'll call Kurosawa-san.[3] Kurosawa-san was furious. We'd sold him a promise: major improvements in our product usability. He had made commitments to his team and his management, yet we had failed to deliver again and again. The whole partnership was in question.

It began to dawn on me that this meeting wasn't going to be an update; we had to save this relationship.

> *I thought I was completely ready for this meeting. Now I realized I wasn't. I had been tossed out of a comfortable sense of readiness into a new and scary place where my careful preparation might be completely ineffective.*

It's a twelve-hour flight to Osaka from San Francisco. Leave late morning, arrive late afternoon, rumpled and tired. We took a courtesy bus to the hotel, checked in, and agreed to meet in the lobby in thirty minutes. When I returned to the lobby, Jan had already joined the group. I seem to remember we chose a restaurant in the hotel, probably shabu-shabu.[4] We ordered our drinks; then Jan started.

"Tomorrow is going to be ugly. Kurosawa-san is really unhappy. His manager is leaning on him, his manager's manager is leaning on him. They put a lot of time and money into this partnership and they feel like they have little to show for it. We need to pull some kind of rabbit out of the hat tomorrow or we're in deep trouble."

"What kind of rabbit?" said our division manager. "More licenses, a longer term for the fees they've already paid?"

"No, that's not going to cut it," Jan said. "They've really lost con-

---

3   This name is an alias. I use a number of these in the book.

4   A popular dish in Japan.

fidence in the program. We have to prove to them that this was an anomaly, that we're back on track and they'll be able to start serious testing soon."

"Hmm. Well, I don't have any easy answers," said the division manager. "We'll have to play it by ear. Maybe they'll offer some ideas."

On that note, we retired, in my case to an anxiety-ridden sleep. Were my slides ready for this kind of meeting?

The next morning, our account manager drove us to the Mitsubishi plant and a secretary showed us into a large conference room. Prints decorated the walls—Mitsubishi promotional posters, cherry blossoms, castles, the inevitable Mount Fuji print. The room was warm, much warmer than I liked. Later I was told that this is normal in Japanese offices. Five or six Mitsubishi engineers were already seated, each wearing the same uniform jacket, a tradition I learned is fostered to build team spirit. Introductions were polite but perfunctory. That was not common— normally the Japanese are extremely polite. This group knew what kind of meeting this was going to be.

Kurosawa-san joined ten minutes late. No doubt a meeting with his boss, detailing the acceptable order and means for our execution, had run over.

He didn't waste time. "Jan-san, I hope you have brought better news on your progress than I have heard so far?"

Jan said, "Kurosawa-san—thank you for arranging this meeting. We understand your frustration. We've brought a big team from our head office to explain in detail where we are on each aspect of the program and to hear your feedback on where we need to improve." Jan then introduced each member of the team. More polite but icy nods.

And so we started our ritual presentations, our division manager followed by leaders for various major functions in the program. Each stood up in turn and gave their pitch, dutifully clicking through their carefully crafted slide decks. Each was bloodily dissected. Kurosawa-san wasn't hearing anything new, in his view, that suggested we had seen the error of our ways or were on a path to improvement.

Twisting the knife further, Kurosawa-san broke frequently for discussions in Japanese with his team. Lots of head shaking and sucking in of breath. In our team, only Jan and the account manager spoke Japanese. We watched them. Their body language was not comforting.

As the newest member of our group, I was last in the firing line, under no illusion about how I was going to be treated. Adding to my discomfort, I was in the early stages of a bad cold, the hot-sweats kind of cold, in an overheated conference room. By this time, I was visibly sweating. I must have looked terrified. I was going to go down in flames.

My turn came. Before anything else, I had to get a little more comfortable, a little less overheated. I took off my jacket and tie and rolled up my sleeves. That brought some relief. I later realized that it also provided an effective touch of theater. I did it because I was hot, but to everyone else it came across as "I'm taking your anger seriously. And I'm going to treat it seriously, unlike the formal and scripted presentations you've heard earlier."

In the rush of the moment, I thought, "Every other presentation has been shot down. Why not try something different?" I said, "Kurosawa-san—thank you for your frankness. Obviously, we haven't met your expectations. I want to tell you about what we have been doing to turn that around. I want to check that this approach is consistent with your needs. And I want to have a discussion about where we should improve."

More reinforcement. This isn't a formulaic "yeah, yeah, I get it, you're annoyed." I'm not just going to talk; I'm also going to listen.

On the spot, instinctively, I added, "I brought slides, but I'm not going to use them. I've been living this for months. I don't need slides to remember. Let me walk you through what we've done."

In this new and scary world, I grabbed a magic sword—I ditched the pitch. I had nothing to lose. Marching through my pitch would have led me into the same pit of torment as my colleagues. Maybe doing this from memory would show my commitment.

Risky move. I had to remember a lot of my pitch. But it meant they had to listen to me; they couldn't read ahead in the slides. And it was more comfortable for them to interrupt—first hear me out on my current point, then question.

"When I first started talking to our engineers, it became clear that they were getting lost in long lists of technical requirements. They didn't see the bigger picture; they didn't know how to prioritize. They'd try to complete as many fixes as they could, starting with the easily fixed issues, which didn't help you much. Then they'd work on a small number of hard fixes, and that didn't help either. To be able to continue your testing, you need all the fixes related to one of your priorities, not fixes based on difficulty. So, we had discussions on which fixes were essential to meeting your highest-priority goals. I want to check this first with you. My understanding is that those are A, B, and C. Do I have that right?"

Because I couldn't hide behind slides, I found I was naturally drawn to describing the process, not just the results. A description in detail of how we prioritized Mitsubishi in the factory. A

> *description of how we understood what Mitsubishi wanted and how we had been working hard to satisfy that objective. Mitsubishi as the hero, the center of attention, not us. Without realizing what I was doing, I was telling the story of our efforts in support of Mitsubishi's quest, not just giving them a status report.*

A short burst of Japanese, Kurosawa-san checking with his team. "Yes, Murphy-san, you have that right." I noticed his mood had thawed a little. He liked that I was involving them in the discussion, talking about their needs, giving them a chance to correct my assumptions. A small victory.

"With that framework, my team took each subgoal in turn. What were the main issues blocking progress? Some in one product, some in another, some in the coupling between those products. We moved resolving those issues to the top of our priorities." I listed some examples from memory. I didn't remember all the details, just enough to be clear I really did know my way around their issues.

"We added up the time each fix would take and how much time we needed for full regression testing, documentation updates, and release. That determined how much we could plan for the next release. We are now working according to this plan for the upcoming release. This will ensure that release will contain all of the following fixes." I listed (from memory) all the check-mark items.

More nods around the table. The next part wouldn't be so easy.

"Unfortunately, when we plan this way, some fix requests you really wanted to see don't make it in." Again, I didn't want to show a slide to illustrate the point, but I offered an example from memory.

> *So far, I hadn't taken any big risks. Now I faced a real challenge. Would Mitsubishi work with me through this challenge or decide they'd rather slice me up like my colleagues?*

A longer burst of more animated Japanese. I guessed that disciplined planning was fine— delaying anyone's favorite fixes, not so much. Kurosawa-san summarized:

"We understand, Murphy-san. The main issue is which fixes have been delayed."

I listed the top three that I remembered would probably be most important. More animated discussion.

Kurosawa-san again: "Murphy-san, we have discussed. We are OK for the second and third points to be delayed, but we need the first in the upcoming release."

"Understood, Kurosawa-san. We will look into whether we can accelerate this issue into the upcoming release, maybe delaying something else, which we would discuss first with you."

Nods around the table again.

Now we were negotiating. Progress.

"Now I'd like to discuss some of the detail behind what we're doing for this release, to get your feedback." I went to the whiteboard and started sketching flows through the tools. "We see typical usage working this way, with these needs…"

You know engineers and whiteboards. Pretty soon, one of the Mitsubishi engineers jumped up, coming to the board and saying, "I can see that, Murphy-san, but have you considered the case when the engineer wants to do this?" And he sketched a variation to the flow.

Another storytelling step—we were on the journey back from that scary world to a more familiar one. I was cementing Mitsubishi's confidence that we were paying close attention to their feedback, reinforcing that in our eyes, they were the hero. We wanted to be in tune with their objectives, to make them successful.

> *I was also drawing them into the story. It is hard for an initially hostile listener to sit on the sidelines, judging, when they have become part of the story.*

That turned into a larger discussion. They weren't just debating with me; they were debating with each other. And I encouraged it. They were involved, and I was listening and taking notes. They were tapped into our product engineering, and we were listening. Out of that discussion came some good insights, for both sides. Now we were talking engineer to engineer—a familiar, comfortable environment for all of us. The dynamic had shifted. What had been two teams sitting across from each other, in an almost adversarial stance, was now a team discussion and brainstorming session.

Eventually, we had to wrap up. I summarized on the whiteboard. There were some small tweaks, and we were done. Everyone thanked me (we didn't shake hands—bad cold). Kurosawa-san thanked me most of all.

I was dazed—partly the cold, partly disorientation. How did we go from my certain slow march to the gallows to all smiles and agreement? After we left the plant, my colleagues grilled me: "How did you do that?" I smiled, shrugged, played it cool; but honestly, I didn't know either. I just knew that marching through my slides would have led to the same unhappy fate they'd suffered. I took a different path—and it worked.

We had dinner that night with Kurosawa-san, still all smiles. His follow-up with his command chain seemed to have gone well. This was a celebration dinner, far from what we had anticipated the previous night. Kurosawa-san capped it off: "Murphy-san, please tell me the kind of food you would most like to try in Japan. Mitsubishi would like to thank you."

I'd always wanted to try fugu, the poisonous pufferfish that can only be served in licensed restaurants. Very expensive. Worth seeing how much they wanted to thank me. Kurosawa-san agreed immediately. The next time we were in town, he would treat me and the team to a full-course fugu dinner. It was spectacular!

TAKEAWAYS

In my early innocence, I had always thought my objective in a sales meeting was to pitch a presentation at my audience—one-way communication, in which I should be the center of attention. This, I later learned, was ridiculously naïve. And yet almost all presentations I see in business still follow that path. The presenter is the center of attention; the audience is in a subservient role. Put that way, it's not hard to understand why most pitches are flops. To break out of that rut, the audience should understand that they are the center of your attention. You are there to serve them and their goals. Your pitch has value only to the extent that it satisfies their objectives. If it isn't meeting their needs, you must take a different path.

In Osaka I chose not to use the pitch, instead stumbling into telling them the story of how we'd been working on their priorities, which proved to be very powerful. I showed them how important they were to us in a way that no status update could have showed. I threw away the script (my slides) because all earlier presentations had bombed. I tapped my instinctive understanding of storytelling, describing our progress in understanding and prioritizing their needs. Ditching the slides and telling a story was the smartest thing I've ever done in a customer pitch.

I still prepared. I still had slides, because some audiences want to see the slides. But I was able to tell my story without them, because in developing and polishing them I had unconsciously memorized most of the important points.

Am I seriously suggesting you have to memorize your slides? It's actually not that hard, if your story is well-structured. I didn't make any special effort to memorize my slides; I never thought I would need to do this from memory. I simply tapped what I remembered from developing the deck. If that seems hard, think of a pianist. She isn't superhuman. She doesn't memorize every note in her sheet music. She memorizes structure, themes, and transitions. Muscle memory takes care of the detail. In your stories you can do the same. Memorize the structure and the main points you want to deliver. If you've reviewed sufficiently before the meeting, much of the detail will come back to you as you talk through the story.[5] What you don't remember probably wasn't that important anyway.

An oral story is the perfect way to start and stay plugged in to what your audience wants to discuss. You can go all the way with no slides, as I did. Or you can use a few visual slides as an evocative backdrop for your story, as John suggested in the foreword. Stay away from bullets and tables and complex diagrams. The slides should support your story; they should not be the story. Use notes if you need to remind yourself of the key points you want to make. Glance down to check the next point in your notes, but keep most of your attention on the audience. Watch their reactions—a nod of agreement or a look of puzzlement—so you'll be ready to invite their input as needed. You're having a conversation, not delivering a monologue. Clarify points they don't fully understand, something you can only do if you are ready to veer off script when needed, to turn a presentation into a conversa-

---

5   Conversely, if the story is difficult to memorize, it probably doesn't have a clear structure. Which will be just as apparent to your audience. Might want to think about that.

tion. Share background on how hard you're working to deliver to their expectations, and show how important their priorities are to you, even if you don't always get it right.

A slide deck is a means to an end, not a recital you must deliver no matter what the circumstances. You should be looking at the audience most of the time, not at your slides, ready to switch from a story to a conversation whenever needed.

REVIEW

An oral story can help you win or regain the confidence of your audience. It should be your go-to form of communication, not just what you fall back on when your laptop won't sync with the projector. It's there for you when you're sitting next to a potential customer or investor, at an event or on a long plane flight. There's an additional benefit. Your audience will be impressed when they see you speaking without slides.[6] That sets you apart from other presenters, as I've found. That's worth remembering if you're in any way ambitious and want to be more than a face in the assembly line of presenters.

Stories can soothe, they can inspire, they can excite in ways that a pitch cannot.

Stories can soothe, they can inspire, they can excite in ways that a pitch cannot. More than that, our audience will remember them long after the pitch is forgotten, because we're all hardwired to remember stories. A story sticks with your listeners, ready to reemerge when they're wondering which vendor to select, in which

---

6   There's nothing wrong with a cheat-sheet of notes. Something you can glance down at now and again. As long as your attention is mostly on the audience.

venture they want to invest, which product they should look at more closely, or which company they should buy.

The tactics I learned from my Mitsubishi experience taught me valuable lessons. But what I didn't learn was a strategy to create compelling stories. What is the magic a story has to draw in a listener, make her eager to learn what happens next, inspire her to expand her goals … and to think that you might be a worthy ally to help her in that quest?

As we'll explore in the next chapter, that proves to be an ancient and powerful magic.

CHAPTER 2

The Architecture of a Story

*W*hat is it about good stories that makes them work? There's a flow to a story which authors, screenwriters, and TV executives know well. A flow that transcends cultures and time, from the very earliest storytellers to modern movie epics, from Confucius to Geoffrey Chaucer to James Cameron. Most important for our purposes, that flow works just as well in our business lives—in sales, investment, growth, marketing, and exits. The flow has power across this incredible range because it has evolved through hundreds, even thousands of generations of hearing and telling stories. We are fine-tuned to communicate in this way. It's in our DNA. Wherever, whenever, and whatever the message might be.

What is this magic spell? To explain, I'm going to pull a dirty trick on my fellow techies. I want to introduce you to a theory from comparative mythology, a decidedly nonengineering discipline. Brace yourselves: we're leaving the realm of mathematical precision and entering the domain of myth and human emotion. I promise to make it as painless as possible.

This hypothesis was developed in the mid-twentieth century by a professor of literature named Joseph Campbell in his book *The Hero with a Thousand Faces*. He concluded that a common structure runs through the myths and stories of different cultures throughout human history, a structure he called the *Hero's Journey*. What's amazing about this journey is how easily we recognize it in many of the popular stories we already know so well: *Star Wars, The Lord of the Rings, Indiana Jones, Harry Potter,* and, well, most of the stories that have gripped us from childhood onward.[7] We can find the same pattern throughout literature, iconic and popular, and in TV shows, comics, and songs. The Hero's Journey is intrinsic to all these stories. Campbell didn't create it; he uncovered it.

In business, sales professionals have always understood the power of a story. They may not all know the Hero's Journey, but those who don't would be surprised to see how well it corresponds with the stories they already tell. In the twenty-first century, the marketing world has woken up to the power of the Hero's Journey.[8] Such stories aren't just valuable in the informal setting of a sales conversation; they work just as well in a presentation to an audience, in webinars, or in blogs.

When we listen to a business pitch, we don't switch to a different

---

7   George Lucas said in an interview that " ... It was very eerie because in reading *The Hero with a Thousand Faces* I began to realize that my first draft of Star Wars (followed similar themes)."

8   Search for "Hero's Journey marketing." Google found nearly 2 million hits when I checked.

mechanism to process what we hear. We have one brain, already trained to resonate with this universal pattern. It wants to hear stories, which to us entrepreneurs may seem odd. We're so accustomed to plodding through PowerPoint product, investment, and status pitches. That's the business standard for communication, isn't it? Billions of words have been written on the uniform awfulness of our presentations. But this isn't a tool problem; it's a message problem. A technical data-dump message doesn't excite a resonance. Resonance requires a real story, built around the Hero's Journey.

Campbell captured the structure of the journey in a diagram, a version of which I have reproduced below. I'll refer to this frequently throughout the book. The journey follows twelve steps along a path from an ordinary world into a special world and then back to the ordinary world. In business terms, a journey from a comfortable, unchallenged starting point, through challenging growth, and back to where you started, though now as a better version of your earlier self. This should sound familiar, but it's much more than "here's your world before and after using my product," as you'll see.

STASIS
Comfortable in the status quo

CALL TO ADVENTURE
A new opportunity appears

CALL REFUSED
Second thoughts

MEETING THE MENTOR
Guidance, encouragement

CROSSING THE THRESHOLD
Commit, no turning back

TESTS, ALLIES, ENEMIES
Tentative steps in new world

APPROACH INNER CAVE
Prepare for a big trial

ORDEAL
Facing the trial

REWARD, SEIZING THE SWORD
A victory, gain abilities

THE ROAD BACK
Return to ordinary world,
face final challenge

RESURRECTION
Apply new abilities, final victory

RETURN WITH ELIXIR
Return home, stronger, more capable

Ordinary World

Special World

THE HERO'S JOURNEY

Rather than detail these steps abstractly, I'm going to explain the journey through another business story—a story as real as all the other stories in this book. This journey is an exciting example John East[9] shared with me, one which serves well to highlight the successive stages along the Hero's path. I'll introduce John soon.

* * *

In early 2003, NASA was putting the finishing touches on its Mars rover program. They would land two rovers designed to roam across a planet that has captivated our imagination as far back as the Babylonians. The rovers were designed to photograph this alien landscape and run serious experiments on the Martian surface. This voyage would be historic—mankind's first up-close exploration of another major planet.

NASA contracted out building the Mars rovers to the Jet Propulsion Laboratory (JPL) in Pasadena, California. Among many decisions JPL had to make in building these complex vehicles was how to control a lot of the functions on the rovers. Sometimes software is a very flexible way to provide that control, but not always. Sometimes you want to use hardware—chips—for faster response times and lower drain on the batteries.

Program managers decided they wanted to use programmable chips for some of these functions, and their preferred choice was chips from Actel. Their chips were known to be better suited to operating under harsh conditions than other similar products. Actel had a proven track record of working well in the space and nuclear

---

9   Core story adapted with permission from a story John first published in SemiWiki.

industries where this extra reliability is very important. Under the cosmic ray bombardment that the rovers would experience in space and on the surface of Mars, that level of reliability was essential.

John East, the CEO of Actel, had been running a successful business for many years selling these programmable logic chips. In early 2003, Actel announced their RTSX-A family of products aimed directly at the satellite market. They'd been shipping prototypes of these devices for a while. For JPL and NASA, the release of this new product line was well-timed. These RTSX-A devices appeared to suit their needs perfectly.

> In the context of Campbell's framework, John started in **stasis** in his **ordinary world**, everyday life, building and selling chips. For a familiar parallel, think of Star Wars. Luke dreamed of adventure but still worked on his uncle's farm on Tatooine.

JPL built four rovers using the Actel chips. Spirit and Opportunity would go to Mars; the other two they kept in a sandbox in Pasadena to help debug any problems they might experience during the mission on the planet's surface. Spirit launched on June 10, 2003. Opportunity launched a month later. Each would take about eight months to get to Mars. Playing a part in this mission was a cool win for John to share with friends and colleagues. Actel in the Mars rovers! We all dream of space exploration, but few of us get to be a part of the reality.

Shortly after the launch, Actel started to get reports from other customers—a few RTSX-A devices were failing burn-in testing in their labs. Burn-in is a test to verify that a chip which starts out functional will stay that way after being in normal use for quite a while. Testing chips for one week at very high temperatures is the standard way to ensure that they'll work correctly for a long time at expected operating temperatures.

> *Here John was **called to adventure**. Not a fun call. An alarm call. An exciting win had flipped into a scary problem. Actel was going to have to step up. We've all been there. In* Star Wars, *Luke met Ben (Obi-Wan) Kenobi, who invited him on an adventure. In some stories, the **call may be refused** at first. The hero has second thoughts. Luke initially refused to follow Obi-Wan, thinking of his responsibilities to his uncle. John didn't have the luxury of second thoughts in this story.*

Actel hadn't seen any failures in its own testing, but when its executives heard these reports, they took a closer look. They ran burn-in tests on around a hundred devices at a time and started to see a few failures—occasionally. Sometimes they'd see one or two failures. Sometimes none.

This was bad—very bad. Electronics can't be repaired in deep space. If one chip fails, the whole mission could fail. Worse yet, there wasn't just one RTSX-A part in each rover. There were thirty-eight. Thirty-eight for each rover, any one of which might fail. Maybe this chip would be OK, but that chip wouldn't. Thirty-eight rolls of the dice, and only one had to come up bad for that rover to die or be severely compromised.

Something was wrong, but John and his team had no idea what. Even worse, other programs were also planning to use these parts. Word got around the space community. JPL heard about the problem. Their mission was already underway. Other customers weren't sure if they dared launch their satellites. All wanted John to tell them that it was OK, that somehow this wouldn't affect their programs. He couldn't. He didn't know what was wrong, and he didn't know what it might affect.

*Our hero had to **cross a threshold** into a **special world**.*[10] *This was a point of no return. John couldn't back out. He had to go forward, to deal with the possibility that problems in his chips might jeopardize the Mars rover mission. Worse still, multiple customers could have been affected. This was now a battle for the reputation of Actel. You'll recognize the same point of no return for Luke in* Star Wars. *He returned to the farm to find his family killed, the farm destroyed. He had to take a different path; there was literally no way back.*

A few skeptics thought the Actel team might be covering something up. That should sound familiar. Even in rational technology communities, there are conspiracy theories.

*A little later in Campbell's cycle we see a test, allies, and enemies. Here we see a hint of **enemies**, maybe some who might have hoped to steal Actel's space business, others who simply see conspiracies in any setback. Think of the famous cantina scene in Mos Eisley, where Luke is surrounded by potential enemies. He and Obi-Wan met Han Solo and Chewbacca, key allies in their quest. John was about to gather his own allies.*

Soon, John got a call from Bill Ballhaus, the CEO of Aerospace Corporation. Aerospace Corporation is a federally funded operation which specializes in providing technical guidance and advice on space missions. Dr. Ballhaus asked John to come to the Aerospace headquarters in El Segundo to discuss "the reliability problem with the Actel chips."

Actel engineers were working their tails off, sixteen hours a day,

---

10   Meeting the mentor comes before this step in the diagram. You should realize that the Hero's Journey is a guideline, not a rigid structure. Some events can move around a little, some might not appear.

seven days a week, trying to figure out what might have caused those failures and whether they might affect the rovers. Unfortunately for the Actel team, nobody cares how hard you're working when you might be responsible for a big problem.

John knew this meeting wasn't going to be fun. The invitation read like a one-on-one with Dr. Ballhaus, so John was thinking of going on his own. But his VP of Technology, Esmat Hamdy, saw it differently. As the CEO, John was the right guy to lead the discussion, but Esmat knew John would need his technical expertise at some point. Esmat strongly recommended that he join the meeting. John agreed without hesitation.

> *In this story, Esmat was the **mentor**—the Obi-Wan to John's Luke. Esmat had powers of technical understanding which John readily agreed exceeded his. Esmat would use those powers to support John in the trials ahead.*

They flew to LAX and took a quick cab ride to Aerospace, a large campus about a mile from the airport. A secretary led them into a huge conference room. A long table ran down the middle, seating fifteen or twenty people. Around that was an aisle, and around the aisle was an elevated area with maybe twenty or twenty-five chairs circling the table below. This was not a one-on-one. John offered a silent prayer of thanks that Esmat had insisted he come along.

> *John and Esmat were approaching the **inner cave**, preparing for the key trial—like Luke entering the cave of evil on Dagobah or being pulled onto the Death Star.*

All the chairs, except for four, were taken by PhDs, experts in every aspect of semiconductor chips that you could imagine. As John modestly put it, technical wizards with at least double his IQ. One of the empty chairs was for Dr. Ballhaus, one for Esmat, and one for John. They took their seats.

The last chair was for a high-ranking air force general who'd invited himself to the meeting. He was running late. When he got there, crisp uniform, tight crew cut, and a chest full of ribbons, there must have been ten minutes of shaking hands, trading laughs. This was a man who was not only respected and even held in some awe, but well-liked. Still, behind that genial exterior was a hint of steel— he was quickly moving through the group, a man with a mission. He didn't get to that rank by just being one of the guys.

> *Now they were in **the inner cave**, facing the **ordeal**. Luke and team were captured by the Death Star, yet were able to sneak aboard unnoticed. Time for Luke to face his enemy, Darth Vader, and test his mettle. John was about to meet his own moment of truth against an intimidating character who might hold Actel's future in his hands.*

The general sat down, opened his briefcase, and pulled out a bundle of files.

"So, Mr. ... er, er ... " the general shuffled through his papers, "... East, is it? You wanna tell me why we didn't just launch $800 million of scrap metal toward Mars?"

John coughed, shifted from side to side in his chair, ran a finger round his collar. The general wasn't done.

"Mr. East. I want to be sure you understand that this is not just about the Mars rover mission. We also have several military satellites planning to use your chips." He punched his finger at John. "And let me tell you something, mister; our nation's defense depends on those satellites. They're not going to launch unless you convince me you've fixed the problem. If they don't launch, today is going to be a walk in the park compared to our next meeting."

> *The ordeal intensified. John already knew the problem would affect satellites, but the general made sure the stakes were crystal clear. Not only was Actel's reputation at risk with NASA, they could also lose the faith of the US government. This was a very high-stakes challenge. John's survival and the survival of his allies hung in the balance. In* Star Wars, *our heroes had to battle through fierce opposition to rescue Leia.*

John prayed for an earthquake, a fire, a medical emergency, anything to buy him time. None of these were on offer. They had to talk their way through. Clearing his throat, he started.

"We understand your concern. We are just as concerned as you. We've been working night and day to test our parts under the most extreme reliability tests. We've talked with the JPL engineers. We've also reproduced failures, so we know it's not something special about your setup.

"I wish I could tell you that at this point we've figured out what caused the problem, but the honest truth is that we don't know. We're still looking, trying to isolate the problem. I'm sure we'll find it, but we're not there yet."

John told me later that he had been terrified. He had to tell the truth, but doing the right thing didn't make it easy. He told them Esmat could explain the testing they had done so far, and that they'd welcome any ideas or help that Aerospace had to offer. Esmat is the guy you want on your side in this kind of meeting—calm, polished, an obvious equal to all those PhDs.

> *The mentor showed his worth. Obi-Wan lent his experience*

> *and power, distracting Darth Vader so the Rebels could escape (happily, Esmat emerged alive from his encounter).*

Esmat explained all the many tests they had already run—variations in programming the device, the voltage they'd used, the length of time the voltage was applied during programming, and the number of times they'd repeated this process. This was like perfecting a recipe—you wanted to get the ingredients just right. They ran lots of experiments, changing the recipe a little bit each time and repeating the burn-in tests.

They were also starting to experiment with another manufacturing facility. Esmat explained all the variations they had tried. But so far, no breakthroughs.

Dr. Ballhaus jumped in. "You know, we have a lot of smart people here and state-of-the-art diagnostic equipment, like scanning electron microscopes.[11] Could we help in some way?"

John grabbed that lifeline. "Dr. Ballhaus, that would be fantastic! As Esmat said, we're doing a lot of testing, we're working systematically through possible causes, but it takes time. We don't have access to the kind of equipment you have. If your team could help us, I'm sure we could get to a solid diagnosis much faster."

> *John was gathering more **allies** to help him in his quest—Esmat, and now the Aerospace team. John wasn't going to overcome the challenge on his own. He needed allies, just as Luke needed allies.*

They worked up a plan; then John and Esmat flew back to San

---

11   Advanced microscopes that are very useful in looking at the small structures in semiconductor designs.

Jose to lick their wounds and get back to work.

On January 4, 2004, Spirit landed on Mars. The press was ecstatic—the first vehicle to land on another planet. Spirit was going to take lots of great pictures and send back priceless data from experiments on the planet's surface; we'd all finally get to see what Mars looked like up close! This was science fiction come to life. The dramatic pictures and the press coverage had the world on the edge of its seat. Spirit started up just fine! It was front page on every newspaper. John and his team breathed an enormous, collective sigh of relief.

Then, on January 21, every newspaper blared on the front page: "Spirit Fails!" The rover had worked for a couple of weeks and then shut down. NASA engineers didn't know what was wrong: software, other components, maybe the Actel chips.

John fell off his chair. He was terrified—again. What if this was Actel's fault? It might have been. The media would have a field day. No news sells like bad news—a massive taxpayer investment down the tubes, and they'd be front and center in this disastrous failure. John imagined lawyers rushing to file suits, process servers skulking in the bushes waiting to spring out and serve him with subpoenas, another meeting with the general.

*The **ordeal** continued. The challenge seemed to have peaked in the Aerospace meeting, but they weren't out of it yet. Real challenges are hard work, not fixed with a single swipe of a lightsaber. Luke and the Rebels fought their way back to the Millennium Falcon.*

The Actel team just put their heads down and kept going, experimenting and testing, experimenting and testing, trying to isolate and eliminate the reliability problem. By April 2004, they were starting to get results on parts made in the second manufacturing facility. Actel and Aerospace were both testing those second-generation parts, and the first-generation parts made in the first facility, each in every possible way. The second generation looked good—really good. The occasional failures disappeared. Nobody knew why yet, but this was promising. Still, future chips wouldn't help the Mars rovers. NASA still had to figure out why Spirit had stopped working.

Debugging a problem in space is hard. Because it's hard, NASA has built immense experience over many complex missions—designing in backup communication channels, diagnostics, work-arounds. They know what can happen, what has happened, and what they can do to work through problems.

First, they lost all contact with the rover. A day later they started to get intermittent communication. Then they got to work. Over the next eleven days, the NASA team worked through each issue, first through a painfully slow link, later through a fast link as they were able to bring that back online.

Through more debug, the team concluded that a lot of the system was working correctly but the flight software was forcing continued resets in the rover electronics. After more debug and more experiments, the NASA team figured out some changes in the software, then erased and reformatted the flash memory. Spirit started working again just fine. Normal operations resumed February 5. The same fix could be applied to Opportunity as soon as it landed.

John finally allowed himself to exhale. The rover mission was on again, at least for now. So far, Actel was not part of the problem. NASA ultimately traced the misbehavior to a software problem, a problem in file management. After the software fix, everything worked as expected.

> *Finally, John got a **reward**. The rovers were working. There was no problem with the Actel chips. Luke and his companions found their reward in being able to escape with plans to the Death Star.*

Most important to John, no hardware problem was found in the Mars rovers. Actel's chips and all the other hardware on the rovers worked just fine. For a long time, John still worried. What if something went wrong on the mission? Was there a hardware glitch lurking out there, waiting to undermine him yet again? Only when both the Spirit and Opportunity missions were well underway did he really feel he and his team were off the hook.

> *Now John was on **the road back**. The drama of the rover failure was over. Actel has been tested and found worthy. They were a proven reliable partner to JPL and NASA. In Star Wars, Luke and the Rebels returned to their home base.*

In the meantime, Actel was feeling more and more comfortable with their second-generation chips. By August 2004 they were able to deliver samples to customers to start their testing. That took some time—mostly sorting out problems with the new programming recipe, making sure it all worked with the various different programming setups in use among all their customers. But the Actel team knew these were chips that had been tested under fire like no others.

> *This was the **resurrection**. John had conquered the intermittent reliability problem thanks to these second-generation chips. He could now claim complete victory—success on Mars and an even more reliable product, ready for any space application. Through his trust in the Force, Luke destroyed the Death Star.*

By the beginning of 2005, all of Actel's customers were happy that the new parts were problem free. The dust had settled. The Mars rovers went on to complete long and successful missions. Now all that anyone remembered was that Actel was the company you worked with if you wanted the resilience needed to stand up to space travel. One of the Actel engineers later bragged that Actel devices were on board every lander that made it intact to the surface of Mars. They'd earned the respect of the space industry and (most likely, though that story remains top secret) the military.

> John and Actel **returned with the elixir**—tested and proven on one of the most advanced space programs of the time. The reliability question mark was resolved. They were now back in the ordinary world, stronger and more widely respected for their capabilities. Luke finally understood and embraced the Force. Because he faced the challenges and rallied his allies around him, he had become a much more powerful version of that boy who left Tatooine and accepted the call to action.

TAKEAWAYS

Stories speak to us, influencing us in ways that a pitch never can. Can you use the same magic in your story? It's quite easy once you learn to tell the whole story, not the usual "life before and after adopting my product" pitch. I'll illustrate through a very common experience, a journey from sales prospecting to delivery. This book is about business-to-busi-

Stories speak to us, influencing us in ways that a pitch never can. Can you use the same magic in your story?

ness relationships, so our prospective customers already have a very good idea of what they want to accomplish. What they don't know is whether you and your skills can help them in that quest. When you meet such a prospective customer, they're going to be in stasis in their original world, at least with respect to you. Just kicking tires.

Your objective is to introduce them to a new and special world in which they can meet their goal in a much more compelling way than they had previously imagined—not just checking a box on their to-do list, but expanding their view of what could be possible. The call to adventure. They may jump immediately at this new and exciting possibility. Or they may initially reject the call. "This sounds complicated and risky. We want something much simpler." We've all been there. Later, maybe they realize they shouldn't have turned you away so quickly, and invite you in for another discussion. You set their minds at ease about the risk, because you are an experienced mentor. You've been down this path many times; you can help them through the challenges.

At some point, your prospect, now your hero, commits, and you both cross the threshold from that earlier, safe but not very ambitious world into a risky and special world where you will both have to stretch. Your hero can't turn back, and neither can you. They are committing time, staff, and money to this direction, losing opportunities to work on other possibilities, which might be disastrous if this adventure doesn't work out. And you talked them into this crazy plan. A little dangerous, but this is where businesses grow and prosper—through calculated risk.

You'll help them gather allies, people who have already advanced their own goals in similar directions, people who can introduce them to other experts in this bigger objective. With your help, your hero will build a prototype, run tests, try a small deployment. Where, of course, they will run into problems, and enemies will emerge. "I told you this would never work. It was a stupid idea from the start." You help them through those problems, justifying the hero's commitment to this direction, at least in a pilot deployment.

Then your hero wants to get serious. "We need to try this out on one of our customers." *Gulp*. Now they're approaching the inner cave. The big challenge. The pilot program shook out a few basic problems, but now your hero hits the ordeal, running into serious problems with that customer. You help them work through those challenges one by one. Eventually the hero completes a successful evaluation with their customer, and they earn a reward, perhaps a commitment to be shortlisted for a big deal.

Your hero is feeling pretty cocky now. They're confident about this new direction and they can simply move back into the ordinary world. Everything that can go wrong has already gone wrong, surely? But there's always a last *gotcha*. Your hero's customer decides to take the system for a more extended spin, or to try it on a particularly difficult case that has always caused them problems. And they run into another problem. The hero knows what to do now. They assemble their team— mentor and allies—and brainstorm. They figure out the answer and get a fix back in short order. This is the resurrection, the hero now proven not only in the initial ordeal but also in a new battle. In the real world, there will always be new battles. The hero's customer now knows your hero is ready and able to handle such challenges.

All is finally well. Your hero is successful, returning with the elixir, now a stronger and better competitor with new and clear differentiation. You, as their mentor, guided them to that bigger and better success.

That's how you tell a great story. A story that will have your next prospective hero asking, "Hey, can you do that for me?"

REVIEW

On my way home from Mitsubishi, I was trying to figure out why my story had been so successful. Now I realize that what I had done, unconsciously, was to tell them a story following the Hero's Journey, based around Mitsubishi's needs and priorities. We started in stasis— long lists of bugs, which we were making some kind of attempt to fix but not in a way that satisfied Mitsubishi. Our call to adventure was to follow the high-level guidance Mitsubishi had already given us. Still in the factory, we entered an inner cave and an ordeal, to debate and get those priorities right. We battled in R&D meetings for approval; we made sure our company was aligned with our plan. In Osaka, I shared all of this with Mitsubishi executives to get their feedback and blessing (the reward and the road back). Finally, I reinforced our commitment through a discussion with their engineering team on use models, double-checking our understanding to avoid future confusion. They happily joined that discussion, which became the resurrection.[12]

Of course, when you're starting out, what you think should be your story may not interest your audience. Then you have to feel your way to a better story. That's the subject of my next chapter.

---

12 I owe you a little clarification here. The story I shared with Mitsubishi was designed for their perspective. In that story, the inner cave and ordeal were our battle with confusion back at the factory. The story I shared with you was told from my perspective. In that story, the inner cave and ordeal were the meeting at Mitsubishi, with them as an unhappy audience.

CHAPTER 3

A Startup Story

I n his book *On Writing*, the famous horror writer Stephen King takes a rare step away from fiction to write about the art of storytelling itself. The second half of the book describes his observations and principles on crafting stories. I was surprised by his views on the premise for the story: setting, opportunity, characters, objective, conflicts, outcome. All the factors that make a story unique. I had always imagined that an author would first lay these out, maybe in the Hero's Journey structure, then start filling in the details. They might tweak things as the story evolves, but the premise would remain more or less secure. Stephen King blows up that idea:

I want you to understand that my basic belief about the making

> *of stories is that they pretty much make themselves. The job of the writer is to give them a place to grow (and to transcribe them, of course).*

Which, from a business perspective, sounds quite similar to a startup story. You aren't quite starting from a blank sheet—you have technology experience from your previous company, or experience from previous successful ventures. That's all you bring to the table. The rest of your story is still to be written. You have to find investors, strategic advisors, and mentors who will help you thread a path toward a successful venture, but it's impossible to plan every twist and turn of that journey in advance. You need to give your story a place to grow.

Here I'm going to share an example of a story that Dave Kelf, a fellow Brit, told me. I was recently reintroduced to Dave by Jim Hogan (whom you'll meet in the next chapter). I'll never forget that meeting in an unassuming office park in San Jose. Dave is a natural and prolific storyteller, excited even when seated, rocking his chair forward and back, arms waving, reliving the story he's sharing. Dave's story provides a perfect example of how Stephen King's guidance applies equally well to startup stories.

* * *

Dave Kelf and Phil Moorby have been friends for a long time, working in and around the semiconductor industry. Phil has been showered with honors for creating new standards in chip verification. Dave's talent is in business development, guiding multiple software startups to strong market positions, many leading to successful acquisition.

Over the years, Phil has built unique expertise in optimizing software to run as fast as possible, especially on computers supporting parallelism, a topic we'll visit soon. At the time this story started, they both had stable, well-paid positions at the same software company.

> *Dave and Phil were in **stasis** in the ordinary world. Comfortable but unchallenged.*

In 2006, Dave decided he was hungry to start a new venture—with Phil. Phil initially resisted. Why give up a comfortable, secure job to jump into a risky venture with no guarantee of success? His wife had the same question. Dave, great salesman that he is, talked them into a change, and they launched Sigmatix. Their product would be a parallel software compiler. This was back when multicore processors were becoming popular. A PC using one of these processors could run multiple software programs in parallel with no loss in performance. Programs could run with no modification to their software. The operating system (Windows, for example) took care of managing which program ran on which core.

> *Dave provided the **call to adventure**, and Phil initially **refused the call**. After Dave talked Phil into the change (and their wives bought in) they quit their jobs and started the new company. They crossed the threshold. That was their point of no return.*

Clever software developers like Phil already knew they could build on this idea. They would break their software into pieces which could run in parallel on a multicore PC, and their programs would run much faster. They'd be able to handle harder problems, be more competitive, and make lots of money by racing ahead of others who hadn't yet tried this trick. That's where parallel compilers come in. These are software compilers, essential in compiling individual programs for multicore systems. As we now know, Phil had a lot of expertise in this area.

What should their story be? They would sell software compilers for multicore systems, but to whom? Software development is a big market, but selling compilers to general software developers is tough. They don't expect to pay for such tools. There are huge libraries of well-known, well-proven and free software for them to use. Dave and Phil weren't going to make any money there. What other customers could they chase? Who should be the heroes in their story?

Dave had a friend in England working on sonar for Trident submarines. In this work he used digital signal processors, known as DSPs. DSPs are specialized processors, able to provide a lot of parallel processing to applications like sonar, audio, and communications, all of which depend on high levels of parallelism. This friend pointed out that open-source tools aren't useful for DSP software development, so the chipmakers provide their own specialized compilers. These compilers are good, but better is always possible, and might be attractive. Maybe these chipmakers would be interested?

> *Dave found a **mentor**. He's pretty good at finding mentors and allies, as you'll see.*

This sounded more promising. Dave and Phil had to prove their compiler on a real DSP application. One of the hottest areas to try was among companies targeting the latest wireless communications standards.

> *Here Dave and Phil had been offered a hint about how they might adapt their initial story. But in storytelling terms, they hadn't yet solved their central problem. They didn't have an identified hero. They were adapting their story to an imagined*

"market hero," but individual heroes and their needs are often more complex.

Around that time, a new standard for cell phone communication, WiMAX, had been proposed. Dave found a company, which I'll call Rtech, building a DSP-based product for WiMAX. Rtech was busy working on its DSP chip and hadn't yet built its own compiler. Its executives were interested in an evaluation.

They provided Phil with the latest revision of the application software and a software prototype of the Rtech chip. He ran these through the parallel compiler, got the software debugged and optimized, and ran the communications test suite, all on a PC. It ran fast—so far, so good.

When the prototype DSP chip was ready, Phil compiled, this time running on the chip rather than on a PC, and reran the tests. That also ran fast, although not as fast as his original PC-based compile. Think about that. Sigmatix's purely software-based WiMAX solution was faster than the DSP chip-based solution—faster than the chip that Rtech was building. Sigmatix had unintentionally overtaken its customer.

The evaluation wrap-up meeting was uncomfortable. Rtech's business strategy was built around their DSP chip as the core technology, not a software solution that didn't need the chip. Not surprisingly, Rtech lost interest in working with Dave and Phil.

*Rtech was definitely not a hero that Sigmatix could help in their journey. This was a **test** for Sigmatix, an early battle in which our hero tried out their weapon (the compiler) for the first time. Dave and Phil met with initial success, but ultimately failure because their weapon didn't match Rtech's needs. This was a part of their training in which they failed, a necessary step in learn-*

> *ing, like Luke in* Star Wars, *in his first lightsaber training with a remote droid, or in his first battle with Darth Vader in Cloud City, a battle in which he lost his hand and almost lost his life.*

Sigmatix had burned through a lot of their funding to get to this point, with no payback. Dave and Phil's business plan had depended on that deal to top up their reserves. To stay afloat, they needed to raise more investment, so Dave restarted his discussions with multiple venture capital (VC) firms. During that funding drive, they met with Richard, a partner at one of the VC firms.

Richard, who must have been all of twenty-eight, met them in a typical VC conference room—cherrywood paneling, walnut table and chairs, the kind of place that screams: "We live in a world of more money than you could possibly imagine." Richard heard them out, then offered an interesting perspective.

"Let me see if I have this right. You've proven your product on a real test case and showed a huge performance advantage. But you can't sell the compiler to software developers because you can't make money that way. And Rtech don't want to buy it because your software would make their hardware worthless."

"That's right," Dave said.

"Stop and think about that. The Rtech guys were planning on selling their product for millions of dollars, using their specialized hardware. You tell me you can run the same software, on a regular PC processor, much faster than they can. See where I'm going with this?"

Dave's eyes widened. "You're suggesting we could sell the whole WiMAX solution? We did run a lot faster than they could. We've been so focused on selling a compiler. What you're telling us is that we should be selling a communication product rather than a compiler?"

"Exactly."

Dave said: "But we built our solution on Rtech software. We signed a nondisclosure agreement. We can't do that."

"Is WiMAX the only wireless standard out there?"

Dave considered the question. "Well … no, there's another new standard called LTE, just released. Qualcomm[13] has announced their support. With Qualcomm behind it, LTE is likely to be big."

"You haven't signed an NDA with anyone on LTE?"

"No."

"Then I think you know what to do next."

> *Dave and Phil found another **mentor** who pointed them onto the next important phase in their growth.*

The next day, they set to work building their own LTE software. Phil really is very good at figuring out how to get the most out of parallelism in software. Their parallel compiler was important for this task. However, Phil also figured out how to rearrange the structure of the software to squeeze in even more parallelism. When he was done, they agreed they had a pretty amazing LTE product.

Now they had to rethink the right heroes for this story. Like most of us, they started right back where they were now comfortable, pitching to the DSP chip builders. "Here's a really fast LTE package that you can run on your DSPs." They should love that, right? But they didn't. Yes, it was fast, but it didn't differentiate their DSP from any other DSP. They were all chip builders; like Rtech, they each wanted the principal value to be in their chip.

> *Another **test**: more potential heroes prove not to be their heroes. Dave and Phil were unsure of themselves. Did they have*

---

13   Qualcomm is a huge supplier of wireless chip products, used in many if not all of the smartphones available today.

> *the right weapon? Were they using it in the right way? Were they out of their depth?*

Dave was sweating. He'd raised a bit more seed money, but it wasn't going to last for long, and he still hadn't found a promising lead. They just had to make this work somehow or die trying. He turned to his contacts in the wireless business. One of them was invaluable, with strong connections and deep understanding of the market. She got him a spot on a panel at the Mobile World Conference in Barcelona.[14] Maybe he could drum up interest there?

> *Dave found an **ally** who led him to the **inner cave**.*

MWC conferences are held all over the world, the biggest hosted in the Barcelona Convention Center, between the spectacular Sagrada Familia to the west and Mediterranean beaches to the east. Dave found his panel scheduled in a giant, packed auditorium. Other speakers on the panel came from some of the biggest names in the communications business: Qualcomm, Cisco, CEVA, and a few others. Dave felt intimidated. Representing his little startup, he was playing in the big leagues. But he wasn't going to waste the opportunity. One of the topics suited his needs perfectly. Panelists were asked whether it was better for communications to depend on specialized processors or standard processors. It was a performance versus cost question—what are the tradeoffs in using a specialized processor to run faster, and do they justify the added cost?

That question started a lively argument among the panelists. Conference organizers love heated debates. Some of the panelists sold specialized processors and were not so enthusiastic about anyone

---

14   One of the top wireless conferences in the world.

exploring this question too deeply. They had the fastest special hardware solutions, and that was enough. But Dave kept battling on. "At Sigmatix, we can run communications just as fast on a PC."

> *Dave was now in the middle of the **ordeal**, fighting to show the value of the software-only solution. That was what Sigmatix did best, but it was also a threat to the more experienced warriors who surrounded him.*

Another panelist—I'll call him Tom—argued: "No, you always have to use a DSP for maximum performance."

Dave suggested, "Maybe with a DSP you could be a little bit faster. But what about cost? A PC is always going to be cheaper than a DSP-based solution. Is that extra bit of performance on a DSP worth the added cost?"

They debated back and forth until it became clear that Tom was struggling to find a comeback to the cost issue (Dave told me, "I'm never the smartest guy on panels, and I never win those arguments. This was a first!"). Tom eventually conceded: "Look, if what you are saying is really true, you need to have a discussion with this guy at Cisco!"

> *Finally, Dave found a **reward**: independent validation that if he could do what he claimed, there was an unexpected way forward to the goal. When all seemed lost, our hero gathered allies around him and saw a way through.*

Cisco would not have been Dave's first guess as a prospective customer. Purely by chance, they had a need in an area where Sigmatix could be a very good fit—an area in which Sigmatix could give them a competitive advantage.

When you make a call on your smartphone, your phone connects to a nearby cell base station—those cell towers you see everywhere. At the foot of the tower is a big box of electronics. Part of those electronics deals with what is called the baseband, using specialized hardware to transmit and receive radio signals through antennae on the tower. There's also a much smaller baseband inside your cell phone talking to its twin in the cell station through the radio link. What Dave and Phil had was a baseband solution that could run on a regular computer processor, the kind you would find in a PC.

Dave and Phil would have happily sold to whoever might need a software baseband. Why they might need it, for cell phones or cell stations, Sigmatix didn't care. But they were about to learn that the "why" was important. Some parts of the market, the cell phone people, were uninterested in their solution. For them, this was a solved problem. On the other hand, the cell station folks like Cisco had been looking for a solution just like this. They already had a healthy business in connecting between the cell tower and central switching stations. They wanted more, to take over cell station baseband, an opportunity driven by an application need, not a raw technology need. A hero who needed the magic sword that Sigmatix had to offer.

Dave and Phil got their meeting thanks to the Barcelona introduction, and it was a big one—with Fred,[15] the Chief Technical Officer of Cisco's wireless division. On the morning of their presentation, they arrived early and chatted over bagels and coffee served on the hood of their rental car in the guest section of the vast parking lot. Trying to stay cool, Phil said, "We need this, and it feels right finally. If we understand Cisco's problems correctly, then I think we've got what they are looking for."

Dave smiled his big Dave smile. "Phil, this time, I don't just feel

---

15   Another alias.

lucky, I feel good. The trick now, is getting this guy to agree with us before his assistant comes in and calls him off to his next meeting."

They made sure they got to Fred's office a little early. His assistant welcomed them, asked if they needed coffee or water, and suggested they wait in a seating area nearby. They watched the second hand creep around on the wall clock. Fred's PA came back. "I'm sorry, Fred's running a little late. You should be able to join him soon." More agonizing, thinking through possible questions and answers. Finally, the assistant asked them to join Fred in his office.

Fred, a gruff Yorkshireman, was a big important guy with a tiny office, whiteboard covered with scribble, piles of magazines and documents on desks, bookcases stuffed with technical manuals and magazines, a regular engineer's office. As Phil and Dave walked in, he was leaning back in his chair with his arms crossed, the universal brush-off signal. He might as well have opened with "Why am I wasting my time with you people?"

"OK, so tell me what you guys are doing."

"Well, we've got this compiler, and we've got our own software implementation of this cellular baseband."

"Oh, really … " he replied, playing with his nails and checking his phone.

Dave thought: *Oh, God, this is going to be a disaster.* But he kept going. "You know, one of the best things about our solution is that we can run a complete baseband on a regular PC server. We don't need any special hardware."

Fred's head came up. His eyes widened. "What did you say?"

"Well, you know, pretty standard configuration. We can run at a hundred megabits per second.[16] I can even run it on my PC right here." Dave had been pushing DSPs at other prospects, but he

---

16   Really fast at the time.

suspected Cisco might not have that kind of expertise.

"Nah, I don't believe you," Fred snorted.

Phil walked Fred through the concepts: "Here's what we did to all these algorithms; we smashed them together like this. After those algorithms are restructured, we've got these ways to use parallel capabilities on the processor. We have this parallel compiler which can take advantage of those features. All pretty obvious stuff once you take apart the algorithms and put them back together in the right way."

Fred shot out of his chair, grabbed a whiteboard marker, and started to talk about Manhattan. "Let me describe a problem. You're working in the middle of the day in Manhattan, lots of people milling around. You're using a cell phone, you and millions of other people. Imagine the base station capacity you need on Wall Street to handle all those calls and data in the middle of the day. You have massive call volume. Then in the evening it drops to near zero. On the other hand, during the day you have low call volume on the upper West Side. But in the evening, when everyone heads home, it shoots way up."

"Verizon and AT&T have to build these very high-capacity basebands, needed in any given location only for a part of the day. All that peak demand moves elsewhere when the commuters get home. Then they need to support peak demand in the outer boroughs, Westchester, places like that. For standard cell towers, where all the baseband stuff lives in a big room at the bottom of the cell tower, that's a lot of electronics and a lot of investment not being used for long stretches of the day."

Verizon and AT&T were Cisco's biggest accounts. They wanted a better system, where each cell tower needed only the minimum amount of electronics, just enough to get the wireless traffic onto a fiber optic cable. That traffic would then run to a bigger central station, which would pull in and process traffic from multiple towers. The idea was that they'd need only a few of these central stations throughout the greater New York area, maybe one in Battery Park, one in Queens, one in Yonkers. Each could switch between towers, as needed, to serve demand as it moved around the area.

Fred said, "Central stations still need a baseband connection to each tower. The standard implementation requires a lot of specialized DSP-based hardware. Simply moving that hardware from the tower to the central station won't reduce cost; every tower will still need its own interface inside the station."

"We want to use general-purpose hardware," Fred said. "Standard PC servers and our own hardware—as much as possible within these stations, so we can easily switch capacity as commuters move around the greater New York area. Then computing investment would be shared more effectively between towers."

Phil smiled and paused before responding: "Our solution runs on regular PC servers; that sounds like it should fit your needs."

Fred was excited. He saw an opportunity for Cisco to grow into a new business by offering less expensive electronics for these central stations—electronics which would be easy to switch to support demand moving around during the day.

Dave saw the opening and took a shot. "OK, Fred, this sounds valuable to you ... "

Fred confirmed, "If your software can do what you say it can do, this is really valuable to us."

Dave smiled and asked the question they'd waited so long to ask ... "How valuable?"

*The **resurrection**. They had finally found their hero. Not a hero they had imagined when they started, but a hero whose needs* *perfectly matched the special magic they could offer. A hero who saw in them an indispensable partner.*

Now that they understood what made their product special, now they understood their own story, it became much easier to find the kind of companies who needed their guidance and magic to write their stories. Dave and Phil found more partnerships. Nokia Siemens Networks developed a concept called *Liquid Radio*, very similar to the Cisco idea. This also allowed for more economical use of hardware from cell towers through to central switching stations. They immediately signed up.

Cisco described a related problem in the Dallas Cowboys stadium. That stadium has a massive farm of baseband electronics to support all the fans who want to video-stream tackles and touchdowns. Up to a hundred thousand fans streaming at the same time—they need a lot of baseband capacity. But most of the time, there's no game, and that huge investment sits idle. The Cowboys organization wanted to get more value out of their investment by renting out access. But who needed that kind of wireless bandwidth, other than them? A better option would be to rent out regular computing capacity—just another server farm. Which they could do if their baseband hardware was almost all servers. Another good fit.

Raytheon had quite a different application in mind. They wanted a more flexible platform for cellular communications in the battlefield. Standard hardware limited their options, especially when they wanted to spoof enemy traffic. A software-based solution was ideal. They could redesign whatever they needed in the most secure part of their organization. No outsiders had to be involved. They also bought in.

> *Dave and Phil **returned with the elixir**. Once they knew their hero profile, they easily found more.*

TAKEAWAYS

A startup story, like a gripping tale by Stephen King, will evolve as it chooses to evolve. You can guide, but you can't control. One of the best ways to guide is to find your true hero as soon as possible. For a startup, that can be really tough. Many, perhaps most tech startups are founded on the tech: a neat idea to do something very techy in a much better way. Nothing wrong with that, but it isn't connected to the real need of a real hero. You have to search for that hero and their need. Perhaps no hero with this need exists. Which is where it all starts getting a bit wobbly. You talk to your immediate circle of connections. They're not interested themselves but tell you they think they know others who might be. You reach out to that wider circle, find mostly indifference, maybe get lucky with one prospect, which may soon sour.

You're wandering around a dark room, searching for a light switch. Maybe you'll find it before you run out of money, maybe not. Recruiting mentors very early on is critically important, to guide you on your search. They also won't know who your hero should be, but they have a much wider circle of useful connections than you do. Even more important, they have friends who can provide insight into business motivations. For Dave and Phil, mentors were Richard, the VC, and the advisor who got Dave onto the Barcelona panel. Until you find your hero, you should try to think as much as possible in the way a likely hero would. Your heroes want to build much bigger stories, like better telecommunications in Manhattan.

They don't care about parallel compilers or software to run on a DSP. This is where your mentors can help. Listen very carefully to people to whom you are introduced, to learn more about their bigger world and where you might fit. Not to become an expert in their goals, but to know how to identify your potential heroes, and what value you really have to offer. It's often not what you imagined.

As one interesting example of seeking guidance, Dave Millman[17] told me a story about an entrepreneur he worked with many years ago. Dave's goal was to help him find his first heroes. This founder had spun out a venture from his previous company, to design and supply sensors for many possible applications. But he had no clear sense of the most promising prospects. Together, Dave and the founder developed a matrix of possibilities. Dave explored those to narrow down a few of the most promising candidates, which led to a good deal with Coca-Cola. A much straighter path from intent to first success, because that company started early with a strong mentor.

REVIEW

There's a very strong temptation in a startup to build your story around your technology innovation, the kernel of your venture. You assume you will accumulate customers and market positioning around that kernel. Moths will be attracted to your flame. This is an entirely understandable viewpoint. You've solved the 10 percent inspiration part of the problem, inventing the kernel. The business piece, and growing the technology as you add more customers, will be the 90 percent perspiration. A hard slog, but that doesn't scare

---

17   Dave runs BizDev.global and helps high-tech startups find their first customers. I'm not especially plugging Dave, though he does seem to know his stuff. Either way, outsourcing this market and prospect discovery, when you don't know the domain, makes a lot of sense to me.

you. Unfortunately, that view can be wildly wrong. You and your product are a mentor in search of a hero, and you can't cross the threshold into your real journey without finding a hero to help. To find that hero, you need to see their bigger goal and a role you can play in helping meet that goal. This is about business inspiration, not technical inspiration. You won't find it on your own. You probably don't even know what that hero will look like. You need mentors who can guide you along as short a path as possible to find your hero.

> *You and your product are a mentor in search of a hero, and you can't cross the threshold into your real journey without finding a hero to help.*

Another thing you'll have to do is to persuade an investor to underwrite your effort while you're trying to figure this out. We'll see an example in the next chapter illustrating how these goals can overlap.

CHAPTER 4

An Investment Story

I n a chapter on investment, maybe you think I'm going to tell you a story about an entrepreneur looking for funding, or her journey through raising multiple rounds of funding. There are plenty of interesting stories of that type, but here I want to turn the tables and tell you a story from an investor's perspective—a story which shows how an investor can be much more than a bankroll. The right investor can be a mentor who can help you craft a much more exciting story than you can alone. This is the kind of mentor I hinted at in Chapter 3.

Investors specialize in certain types of investment. They accumulate learning from those investments—both good and bad—some of which may be relevant to your venture. Investors also have dreams. Not just to make a return on their investment, but to underwrite something significant—bringing the internet to the third world, reducing poverty, improving healthcare. Some investments work out, most don't, but the investor with a big dream story is passionate about filing away lessons learned on each venture of that type. The best, purpose-driven kind of investor wants to become a Gandalf,[18] who knows where all the opportunities and pitfalls lie and can tell you who might be enemies and who will be trusted allies. They invest for profit, but they also invest to pursue a larger purpose.

I've known Jim Hogan for upwards of thirty years. For about the last twenty, he's been involved variously in institutional investment, seed investment on his own behalf, and investment in and through a semiconductor incubator.[19] Jim has served on more boards than I can remember, contributing to successful exits for ventures in areas as diverse as internet advertising, consumer feedback applications, and semiconductor design. He's quick to add that he's also had his share of failures. This guy is experienced. Jim shared with me a big dream story which nicely illustrates the role of a mentor-investor.

* * *

Many years ago, Jim put money into a seed investment round for a venture called Theranos. The CEO, Elizabeth Holmes, told Jim and other investors a compelling story about her technology—to massively automate blood testing using just fingerprick blood samples. That story captured Jim's imagination and wide attention beyond, including among the upper reaches of the political aristocracy,[20] to

---

18   The wise wizard and mentor in J.R.R. Tolkien's *The Lord of the Rings*.

19   Silicon Catalyst.

20   George Shultz, former secretary of state; Henry Kissinger (ditto); and James Mattis, former secretary of defense, had all served on the Theranos board.

the point where Theranos raised significant investment—as much as $750 million. Everyone was captivated by this young woman, a self-made billionaire who'd spun a $9 billion healthcare company out of a simple idea. She told a story about a technology that could replace expensive tests that must be run in specialized labs and take at least a week to deliver results with an inexpensive, portable test that could be run in your doctor's office, in a field hospital, or in a desperately poor village in the third world. It was a magical idea.

But then in 2015, it all started going wrong. The *Wall Street Journal* published articles citing damning information leaked by whistleblowers. More research showed that results from the Theranos machine were inaccurate and that the advances they claimed had never been properly peer-reviewed. The Theranos story started to unravel and collapsed amid fraud investigations and federal indictments. Jim, along with many others, lost his stake.

Jim and other investors did a lot of soul searching, realizing that important steps had been skipped. Due diligence hadn't been sufficiently broad or sufficiently diligent. They should have insisted on more independent viewpoints along the way. It had been a particularly compelling vision hyped far beyond what it was able to deliver. Jim filed the Theranos debacle away under "lessons learned." You can't skip steps. There is no such thing as growth and success without trials, risk, courageous choices, and the help of allies. There's a reason that the cliché "too good to be true" has such staying power.

Jim told me that he avoids cold calls—entrepreneurs coming to him just to get money. He wants to understand the big-picture concept and the people, and he can't get much of that from a pitch. He also wants to add value—in a board role, certainly, but also in helping the venture along. Like all good investors, he relishes the role of mentor. For him, the best cases don't even start with money. They start with someone in his fairly extensive circle asking him for advice.

One such person was Luke Clark.[21] In the early 2000s, Luke built a small company developing a product for semiconductor manufacturing based on image processing and system optimization. Jim had helped Luke position the company for sale to a semiconductor-equipment maker in Europe.

Luke had been with that company for a while, but he and his wife missed the US and wanted to raise their kids back in the home country. Luke reached out to Jim for advice. "Any ideas on where I could find a job back in the US?" Jim knew Luke was a bright guy, one successful venture already under his belt, so he suggested, "Why don't we figure out something more ambitious than just a job?"

> *Luke was in **stasis** and a trusted **mentor** invited him on an adventure.*

Jim's a master at drawing connections between apparently unrelated experiences. Not long before Luke had contacted him, he had developed kidney stones. He'd gone straight to the emergency room, where they ran a CT scan and found cysts on his kidneys. Not unusual for someone over fifty, but there was a small chance they could be cancerous. However, it was Memorial Day weekend, and the radiologist in Santa Cruz was out for a couple of weeks.

Because only the radiologist could give an expert opinion, Jim had to wait for him to get back. That was a frustrating and anxious time. Eventually, the specialist returned, looked over the scans, and came back with an all-clear: "You're fine." Good news, certainly, but why had Jim had to suffer two weeks of anxiety before he'd had results? There was something flawed about the system—it was

---

21　An alias.

too dependent upon one doctor's availability. His entrepreneurial instinct couldn't help but wonder what the fix, the opportunity, might be here.

Luke had recently lived through a much more painful story of the tragic results of a failure in prompt medical diagnosis. He'd recently lost his mom to deep vein thrombosis on a visit to Belgium. Why couldn't that risk have been detected earlier? They both agreed that Luke's earlier work—image processing and statistical analysis for semiconductor manufacturing—ought to be useful in more quickly diagnosing these conditions. There should be other applications, detecting other cancers, heart lesions. They agreed that this was a path that interested them both, but where should they start?

Jim did a quick market analysis and decided that lung cancer was their best target, because it's the leading cause of cancer-related deaths. The National Institutes of Health conclude that the best way to reduce mortality in these cases is early detection, which depends heavily on MRI and CT imaging. The problem is that cancerous tissue isn't always obvious in such scans, so there's a lot of active research focused on screening, especially in automating early detection as a starting point for more expert diagnosis.

They started brainstorming. Jim asked Luke, "What do we know about MRI and CT scans? We know these produce very complex images, right? That's a lot of data to sort through."

Luke agreed. "Modern semiconductor manufacture is very similar. We have to analyze hugely complex images to detect potential problems.[22] There ought to be parallels."

Jim said, "Yeah—you know, what you've been doing with statistics is sort of like artificial intelligence (AI), applying that to

---

22 Semiconductors are built by printing a succession of images onto a wafer of silicon.

detecting problems in images, right? So, you can detect anomalies in those images?"

"Well ... " Luke paused to consider the point. "I guess I'd say yes and no. What we've all been hearing about with AI, cars detecting street signs and pedestrians, that's a different technology. It's very impressive, but sometimes it's wrong. The problem is that with that style of AI, it's very difficult to figure out which cases are wrong or how to fix them, other than running the AI through a lot more training."

"But that's not so bad, right?" Jim countered. "You overdetect sometimes. If you use it in a car, maybe the car stops sometimes when it didn't need to?"

"True," Luke said. "If it's occasionally oversensitive, maybe that's not too bad—you get an occasional surprise. But you wouldn't be happy if it was slamming on the brakes every five minutes, or worse yet if it failed to recognize a pedestrian and didn't stop. Acceptable margins for error are not that big."

"Fair enough," Jim agreed. "I don't want a cancer detection system to overload the radiologist with apparent cancers that aren't real. They'd just lose confidence and stop using the software. And I definitely don't want to miss real cancers. What do you suggest?"

Luke thought about it. "Well, there's recently been quite a bit of interest in statistical approaches to recognition as an alternative to current AI techniques. Popular AI methods are—I don't know a better way to describe this—kinda magical. When they work, they're fantastic, when they don't work, you have no idea why. Statistical methods are based on well-established math. When they don't work, you can figure out what went wrong and tweak to fix that problem. It's a different approach with some advantages in diagnosing detection problems, providing a way to incrementally improve.

"I want to be clear," he added, "that techniques for recognition are a very hot research area in AI. I don't want to claim statistical analysis is superior. No one yet knows if one method is better than the other."

Jim was jazzed. "Never mind that! I'll bet there are plenty of ventures trying to sell tumor recognition based on conventional AI. We'll have our own approach with clear differentiation. Let's do this!"

*The **call to adventure**! Jim saw an opportunity to steer Luke toward a much more exciting possibility than just "a job." The journey was underway!*

Jim's wife Anne died of cancer many years before this, so he still periodically reads papers on cancer research. He told Luke, "The American Cancer Society has an annotated MRI data set, about a thousand MRIs we can get for twenty-five dollars. We could use that as a starting point to see if this idea passes a first sanity test."

Jim suffered a real loss. The determination and strength born of that grief is a special power he brings to this venture, to share with Luke on their joint quest.

With Jim as the money guy and Luke as the implementation guy, they started. Luke wrote a quick algorithm, using his process optimization ideas on these scans to see if he could detect tumors that had not been detected correctly before. With some help, he optimized the code and filed for a few patents. Jim put in $100,000 for patent licensing and initial research expenses. After about a year, Luke was finding tumors, including some that hadn't been detected previously.

> *Jim and Luke were* **crossing the threshold** *into the* **special world***. $100,000 is real money. They were not just going to walk away at the first sign of a problem.*

This detection was built on 3D scans, which meant they were able to do 3D recognition, something also novel in this area since most AI recognition methods work with 2D images. Using 3D recognition is valuable in cancer detection because there's a critical stage in tumors called vascular growth. This is when a tumor becomes self-supporting by growing capillary structure. 3D recognition can more easily detect that stage. Jim went further by running the image into a 3D printer. A physical 3D model is pretty compelling. Show that to an oncologist or a surgeon, and they immediately understand what they're looking at.

So far so good, but this was still just two guys playing with an idea. Jim wanted some expert validation. As he told me, "I wanted us to talk to expert radiologists, people at universities and major institutions, have them check and validate our stuff. I wanted them to tell us about where they thought radiology was headed in the future and if they thought we could play an important role in that future, get other experts into the mix, to make sure that we're not blinded by love for our idea and to make sure we have good guidance in this field. After all, neither Luke nor I are health experts!"

> *Jim recognized he needed to gather* **allies** *and put this idea to expert* **testing***. When we think we are creating something wonderful, we want so much to be right that we're tempted to skate past difficult problems—skip steps, as Theranos did. Jim was not about to repeat that mistake. He wanted to build an expert team that would question every step. A fellowship, like the one Gandalf gathered at Rivendell in* The Lord of the Rings*.*

To get to this next step, Jim reached out to his network, to Peter Levin and Steve Ondra, whom he knows from Amida, a DC-based company where Jim is an investor and board member. Amida works in data management and exchange in cybersecurity and governance for health, public sector, and other organizations.

Peter is the CEO of Amida and had been CTO for Veterans Affairs (VA) during the Obama administration. Steve is a senior advisor at Amida, earlier appointed by President Obama to be senior health advisor to the VA. He'd also been a professor of neurological surgery at Northwestern University for many years. Now he divides his time between advisory roles in several companies.

Jim invited Steve for a chat out at Jim's home in the Santa Cruz mountains. They sat on the back deck, drinking iced tea and looking out over the forest toward Monterey Bay and the peninsula.

Jim started. "Steve, thanks for coming out here. I want to talk to you about a role in this venture, in fact the lead role. Luke is our tech guy. He has lots of background in the software foundation for this product, and he's been doing phenomenal work. I'm helping through investment and my experience in guiding small tech ventures.

"But neither of us has any real background or credibility in medical tech. You have a ton of credibility, through your career in surgery, your work with the VA, and your advisory work with medical insurance and other companies. Would you be interested in heading up this venture as the CEO?"

Steve smiled. "Jim, you're quite the salesman. Setting me up with a fun opportunity and a great view! I'd guessed that might be why you invited me out here, and yes, I'd be delighted to help. This looks like an exciting venture; could have a big impact. I think I could add real executive value through my understanding of needs in big hospitals and especially in the VA. And, as I'm sure you're well aware"—he grinned—"I can draw upon a pretty sizable network of contacts."

Jim smiled back. "That's a relief. I thought you'd see what a great fit this is, but you never know. Let me test your commitment a bit further. First, we're running on a shoestring. So far, just my investment. I want to avoid any overhead until we're further down the road. No salaries or benefits for anyone. We'll all be paid in equity. Second, I need your help to get expert advice on what costs we're going to encounter, for example in certification, to get to a product we can sell. Third, I'd like you to help in fundraising. We're going to have to pay for those additional costs. Are you still interested?"

> *Jim knew what was coming next in the story. He'd learned that real growth and opportunity involve a series of tests and challenges. He was checking the boxes, making sure they had a plan for each step and that this ally fully understood and was committed to the cause.*

Steve laughed. "Not a problem! I don't need a paycheck. The fun of the venture and the promise of making a little extra if this works, that's enough for me. Contacts are also not a problem; I already have some ideas. And I can help with raising extra capital. I have plenty of friends who dabble in investing. They should be interested, knowing that I'm running the venture."

They shook hands and shortly afterward registered the company as Delineo Diagnostics. Peter also signed on as an advisor. Now this quest had serious medical and business expertise, credibility, and connections behind it.

Steve's first step was to reach out to senior radiologists with banks of data; he's closely connected to radiologists in Chicago and in the Florida VA. He lives not too far from the Orlando VA hospital, one of the biggest in the US. That's important to this story because the VA has an above-average population of smokers. They run scans on all their cancer patients and have a rich database on which Delineo could test their software.

> The team prepared for the tasks that led to **the inner cave**. So far, it had all sounded good, but now they had to prove themselves to cancer experts in some of the biggest hospitals in the US. And they were about to hit roadblocks. Because that's what happens in real stories.

Jim explained the roadblocks to me. "When you're asking an organization for help, there's always a question of what's in it for them. Some places like Berkeley and Stanford are constantly helping startups. They have a streamlined process—a one-page agreement defining what they will get for their help. Review that, sign it, and the work can start.

"The people we'd contacted have experience working with giant companies but not with startups. On top of that, the VA is a government operation and has a lot of safeguards to avoid favoritism. They have to make sure that taxpayers are getting a good deal for any help they provide to private enterprises. There's a lot of process. Everyone has to go through the same process, whether they're General Electric or a piddly little startup like us.

"Which means that first the Chicago hospital and the VA had to generate legal paperwork. What they handed to us were big thick contracts—looked like they stitched them together from a bunch of previous contracts.

"That was ugly," Jim remembers. "I had to hire a team of lawyers to make sure we got it right. I burned forty or fifty hours at a thousand dollars per hour. That was freaking me out for a while, not knowing when we'd be done. But what else are you going to do? If you shop it around, pretty soon word gets out and someone else jumps ahead of you."

> *The **ordeal**. Contracts and rapidly rising legal costs. As Jim understood, there was no going back. Creation, growth, triumph ... they don't come without risk and tests of your commitment. There are no shortcuts on the Hero's Journey.*

They finally made it over the legal speed bumps, and Luke was cleared to travel to Chicago and Orlando to do testing and tuning, prototyping with expert radiologists to make sure the software was meeting their needs. Luke and at times Steve were traveling around the country showing the experts what they were able to do, taking careful notes on what those experts wanted to see improved. Then Luke headed back to home base, to work more on the software and update Jim and Steve on progress (or setbacks). The process repeated, over and over again, until the medical experts told them (with Steve checking very carefully with his medical counterparts) that this software could really help them in early diagnosis.

Luke completed his prototyping work in the last quarter of 2019, with enthusiastic endorsements from both sites.

Steve and Jim knew the next hurdle they'd have to get over would be getting this software certified by the FDA[23]. Jim asked, "What is it we have to prove to get from this stage to a saleable product? I know the FDA has to get involved, but what does that mean? How do we figure this out?"

> *Another **ordeal**. Jim sought out another ally.*

---

23   Food and Drug Administration, the US government organization responsible for approving medical devices, treatments, and drugs, as well as other areas.

Even though Steve came out of the government and military side of healthcare and Peter had worked for many years with the VA, they had no experience with FDA certifications. Steve talked to a friend of his, David Miller.

David was the president of the spine division of Medtronic for many years. He's been through a bunch of these certifications, so he knows the drill—what they expect, the process, the cost. He told them first that what they were building was a diagnostic device. That meant that it wouldn't be as expensive to certify as a drug or an implant, but there was still a process they needed to go through.

*Steve and Jim brought in this new **ally** who could bring them a crucial power required for this decisive stage of the quest.*

"When you add it all up," he told them, "you're looking at about $600,000. And you'll need a letter of recommendation from a major medical institution." A big VA hospital would definitely qualify.

Steve asked for and got the letter of recommendation from the Orlando VA. That part was easy. Meantime, Steve, with Jim's help, was busy raising $600k. They talked to five of their friends and put together a small angel round to cover the cost.[24]

They got those friends excited about the potential scope of the story: not just the lung cancer application, but how their diagnostic tools could be applied to other areas of diagnosis. Since they did analysis on CT scans, frequently full-body scans, they could build on the database they had already seen—to look for heart lesions, brain tumors, almost anything. This was a pretty obvious path to expanding the business later on. Delineo would have to get an FDA certification

---

24 Angels are individual investors. They usually invest very early, before a venture has proven it has a viable product.

for each application with a new incremental cost each time, but the invention and prototyping stages would be much simpler.

> *Here they had to be cautious about an "overly ambitious story" hazard. To investors, they had to show not just the immediate application but how that could grow. Investors want to see room for growth beyond the first product. They want to see the "vision" part of the story. But the vision shouldn't overtake the immediate story. With Theranos, the immediate story was lost in the glare of the big picture story. Jim didn't want to repeat that mistake.*

Steve pulled together enough investors to cover the certification cost. They were ready to start their FDA application. David's help was invaluable here. If you've ever done anything contractual with the government, you'll know that they like their paperwork, lots of paperwork. That was the next hurdle.

> *Another **ordeal.***

There are businesses that specialize in preparing FDA applications. Steve had to hire a couple of those folks—that cost $25,000. But again, there's no way around this. You could try to figure it out on your own, but you might keep getting bounced because you haven't filled the forms out right or you forgot to include other critical forms. Get that wrong a few times and the FDA stops returning your calls.

Steve outlined his discussions with David and the consultants.

"Whatever way we approach this, we should ask for a pre-submission meeting, where the FDA can give us input. Later, there's a final submission, where they make a decision to accept our study and application—or not.

"On the final submission, if they approve the study and our claims supported by the study, we can market our product for clinical trials.

"If they disapprove, we have to go back to the drawing board. That's why the pre-submission meeting is so important. I've no doubt they'll be more careful after their Theranos experience. We need to get their initial feedback before we get too far in. Especially for an area like recognition software for imaging."

They knew that this wasn't going to be easy, but Steve had a plan.

"There are two possible paths we could go down. One is called 510(k). The idea here is to propose that they compare our offering with a "similar" device they call a predicate. The predicate should already have been approved and should be more or less "equivalent" to our product. They'd use that as a reference in analysis of our submission.

"510(k) is the common path for medical devices, treatments, and drugs, but has problems from our perspective. Maybe we could present a GE medical imaging device as a predicate, but those devices are very different from our software. We're not trying to deliver medical imaging. We want to deliver more intelligent analysis of that imaging. But the way the process is set up, the FDA could come back and say we failed to prove equivalence.

"Between us—David, the consultants and myself—we collectively concluded that a better path is an Investigational Device Exemption (IDE). This is designed specifically for a new device. The barrier for software in the IDE path, especially for clinical support, is much lower, nowhere near what we would have to do for treatments, implants, diagnostics, and pharmaceuticals."

"Also, once the FDA accepts the study objectives and protocol in a pre-submission, if we do what they accepted in the pre-submission and it comes out well, they are committed to approval. An IDE approval will allow us to start official clinical trials, which would be a major step forward. It would also establish us as a likely predicate for this domain, which could create a considerable barrier to any competitors."

> *Finally, they were ready. They had invested significantly and shared a lot of equity to get to this point, but now they had the knowledge and experience—their magic sword—to see a clear path forward. This was their **reward**.*

By early April 2020, Delineo sent their pre-submission meeting request to the FDA.

Jim told me that in normal times, they might expect to get certification to move to clinical trials by the summer or fall of 2020. Of course, these are not normal times. The FDA is buried in certifications for COVID-19 tests, treatments, and vaccines of multiple varieties, all while operating under the same constraints as the rest of us. Jim expects a ninety-day delay on their original estimate, pushing approval out perhaps to the winter of 2020.

But not indefinitely. We still continue to have medical problems other than COVID-19, and we continue to want new treatments, implants, and diagnostics. Advances in cancer treatments and diagnosis will continue to be critically important, today and long after we've solved COVID-19. The certification process for the Delineo product will continue, if a little more slowly.

> *As I write this, Delineo haven't yet made it to the **resurrection**, but they're cautiously optimistic. They've done solid due diligence. They have first-class endorsements, and they know they've taken a path with the FDA which is likely to lead to approval. I expect by early next year they will be into clinical trials.*

TAKEAWAYS

The first big takeaway is what a difference an experienced and passionate mentor-investor can make! No trial and error, just a straight path from concept to delivery. In fairness, I don't know how often the stars would align this well for an investor and entrepreneur to connect so seamlessly. The Delineo story isn't finished yet, though there's no reason to believe the FDA approval won't come through. Nevertheless, a mentor-investor can be a heck of an advantage in the story of a startup.

That becomes obvious not only in Jim picking up bills for patents and legal services, but also in his relentless efforts to gather allies. Jim is very much the Gandalf in this story, tasking Frodo to start serious development, then riding off to recruit Steve and Peter. Steve then brings in David. These allies added serious relevant experience and credibility to the team, helping make the right choices at the outset and smoothing the path with the VA, the Chicago hospital, and the FDA. A typical software venture could never have pulled that off on its own.

What made this fast-track startup possible? Jim had seen in Theranos how not to do it. Don't skip steps. Get expert assessment and buy in before going to the FDA. Don't let dreams outrun reality. Steer clear of institutional big-money investors in this case.[25] Insist on expert approval

Insist on expert approval at every step. Do everything the right way and allow for unexpected challenges and trials. Gather the best possible allies to lead the story.

---

25 Big investors can play a very important role. Jim just didn't want them tilting the scale while he and the others nursed this venture to its first wins.

at every step. Do everything the right way and allow for unexpected challenges and trials. Gather the best possible allies to lead the story.

Jim also had a passion to make this story happen—to find a better method to diagnose lung cancer, in honor of his late wife. The path of the great mentor-investor is defined by purpose and intention. Gandalf knew the evil in the Ring and Sauron long before the start of the Ring cycle and had gained great wisdom through that time. He had a passion to prevent that evil at any cost. Jim also had a noble passion and earned wisdom to back it up. That's a potent combination.

REVIEW

Of course, the entrepreneurial journey is exciting, and if you're in it just for the excitement and tales to tell around the campfire, that's fine. But remember that the stories of real adventures are littered with swamps, fire-pits, and dragons. If your story ends in failure, no one outside your circle of friends will care. All that work and angst, and all you'll have to show for it is more debt. If it's important that your story have a decent chance of a happy ending, you should find a mentor-investor, a Gandalf, who's lived a similar story, who knows where to find those pitfalls and when it's time to invest or look for guidance. Find a mentor driven by a fire more intense than a return on investment.

Once you've built your product and got your investment and whatever certifications you need, you're on a roll. You're closing customers and running a profitable business, and life looks good. But that doesn't mean your problems are over. Growing companies still run into challenges. Handling those challenges effectively is also a story that you have the power to craft, a lesson we'll appreciate in the next chapter.

CHAPTER 5

A Growth Story

In 1990, Germany won the World Cup in their third final in three successive cycles. This was a team that had been playing at the elite level in soccer for what seemed forever. They believed, many of us agreed, that they were now a dynasty that could never be toppled. But all dynasties crumble, theirs faster than most. They didn't get past the quarterfinals in the next two cycles, a humiliation they hadn't suffered in a decade. They had to rediscover humility, to reinvest, to learn from scrappy teams far below their previous lofty heights.[26] That hard work ultimately led them back to success—they won the title again in 2014, a reminder that challenges are not just about getting to your first success; they're also about striving for success beyond that first win, getting back on

---

26   The San Jose Earthquakes, for example.

your feet each time you stumble.

Failure is an inevitable part of growth, as the German soccer team realized. But failure isn't simply a bad experience to be endured. As countless motivational posters remind us, we don't learn from our successes; we learn from our failures.[27] Some level of failure is unavoidable if your hero expects you to stretch more than you had planned. When they need you to reach for a bigger goal to meet their goal, you must start your own quest—a quest within a quest.

Peter Calverley is on the Board of Directors of CoolIT Systems. He had stepped in to run the company as CEO just before this story started. CoolIT, based in Calgary, builds direct liquid cooling systems for the servers used in datacenters, the cloud, and supercomputers. CoolIT is an already-successful company that rediscovered the excitement of growth in this story.

* * *

Cray has been synonymous with supercomputing for as long as most of us can remember. Their computers are at the center of solving some of the biggest problems in research, industry, and defense. These supercomputers deliver superior performance through massively parallel computing. They pack huge numbers of processors together into as small a space as possible to reduce communication delays inside the computer cabinet. These computing titans burn megawatts of power and generate an enormous amount of heat, which has to be pulled out quickly. If cooling isn't efficient, the computer must slow down to generate less heat until the temperature falls back below a

---

27 For example: Richard Branson, "You don't learn to walk by following rules. You learn by doing, and by falling over." Or Thomas Edison, "I failed my way to success."

critical level. Slowing down is not a great look for a supercomputer.

Fans can blow air through the cabinets, but that isn't sufficient for these monsters. You can't blow enough air fast enough in such cramped spaces. To increase efficiency in drawing heat out, they also depend on liquid cooling. Liquid flows through copper plates on top of the chips, drawing heat away as quickly as the liquid can be pumped. Cray had already used liquid cooling technology from CoolIT on earlier-model computers. CoolIT was well-established as their preferred cooling partner, and the company was well-integrated with the Cray development team.

Cray is among the supercomputer elite, a many-time holder of the title "fastest computer in the world." They're aiming to regain that position in 2022. Because effective cooling is a limiting factor in delivering high speed, Cray is uncompromising in demanding the best of the best in liquid cooling. It was natural, then, for CoolIT to be in the running to build a new state-of-the-art cooling system to match Cray's new state-of-the-art supercomputer. Late in 2018, CoolIT proposed a complex new system to meet Cray's advanced needs. Through early 2019, Cray hosted multiple engineering visits to their manufacturing headquarters in Chippewa Falls.

Peter told me that arriving in Chippewa Falls is quite an adjustment for anyone based in Calgary, a city a hundred times its size. A couple hours east of Minneapolis, Chippewa Falls is deep in rural Wisconsin, best known to many for Leinenkugel's beer and Oktoberfest. On the outskirts of this hamlet, you'll find the manufacturing facility for one of the top supercomputer makers in the world. A strange location for the company, you would think, until you learn that Chippewa Falls is where Seymour Cray, the founder, was born.

As the project ramped up, the two teams would meet to talk through brainstorming and planning, making sure what they conceived would meet the needs of the next-generation system, yet also be buildable and within budget. They'd go out for dinner after work and continue the debate. One night, Cray hosted them at the best steakhouse in town. It was a great relationship—one harmonious, integrated team.

Cray finally approved the CoolIT bid and funded the prototype phase. The CoolIT folks were excited—a new design and new challenges, the fun part of engineering! If this worked in production, it could drive significant business, and not just with Cray. Peter expected the new design would become a standard in all servers and datacenters. CoolIT would be ideally positioned to take advantage of all that new demand!

> **Stasis.** CoolIT was about to build a new cooling system but was still largely in its comfort zone. It had no reason to believe this project would present any unusual challenges. In this story, Cray was the **hero** and CoolIT was the **mentor**.

Up to this point, CoolIT had handled manufacturing through a contract organization in Shenzhen, China. That partnership was good enough at first for keeping costs down on low-complexity designs, but right after they won the Cray bid, the Trump administration's tariffs on Chinese goods kicked in. Pricing rose because of those tariffs and became a lot less attractive to Cray. And there was another problem. Both companies were concerned about uneven quality in product shipped from Shenzhen. Cray had emphasized that quality was their biggest concern.

CoolIT had already been thinking about bringing manufacturing back from China at some point—allowing them to deliver superior-quality and higher-complexity products direct from their home base in Calgary. Tariffs tipped the balance for Cray—"at some point" had to become "now." This Cray deal would be the lead program to drive the transition.

> **Call to adventure.** *CoolIT would have to move outside their comfort zone. They initially* **resisted** *the call to adventure, wanting to implement the upgrade on a more relaxed schedule. But Cray made it clear that pricing and low quality meant stasis was no longer an option. They wanted CoolIT to speed up the transition to in-house manufacturing for this project—a much bigger goal, and an expectation that would launch CoolIT on their own sub-quest.*
>
> *In* The Lord of the Rings, *Gandalf, the mentor, was also forced to accept more responsibility. He battled the Balrog in the caves of Moria, allowing the others to escape. Gandalf paid a price as he was dragged into the pit of fire. Later he reappeared as Gandalf the White, wiser and more powerful.*

Cray and CoolIT debated the implications and impact on schedule and pricing, and came to an agreement. Cray was happy—pricing would return closer to their bid expectation, and they could have higher confidence in the quality. CoolIT was happy too. They were going to make this change anyway; why not now? Manufacturing at their HQ would be easier to manage and more tightly controlled. Even better, their own plant would give them an advanced manufacturing baseline, a competitive advantage for all future product introductions.

> **Crossing the threshold.** *This was the point of no return. CoolIT and Cray had committed schedules. Going back was not an option. To aid Cray in their quest to push the boundaries of supercomputing, CoolIT had to set out on their own sub-quest, to establish manufacturing in Calgary.*

Cray provided Peter with a forecast—it wanted to start manufacturing in May or June of 2019, ramping to full production in mid-August. Peter learned later that in making commitments to their own customers, Cray had added a two-month buffer on top of these dates. By mid-August, CoolIT had their production line in Calgary set to go, delivering prototypes from the Shenzhen operation in the meantime. Right on track. Time for a celebration, right?

Wrong.

> By now, you've recognized this pattern in every business story. Stephen King again—no story evolves exactly according to the writer's plan. If you're experienced (and I'm sure you are), you'll build some margin into your plan. Even if your plans are built on reasonable expectations, those expectations may prove to be wrong, and the unexpected should be expected.
>
> CoolIT had entered into their own tests, failures, and learning.

A manufacturing plant needs a building, tooling, and staff. It also needs a steady supply of high-quality materials and components to build its finished products. CoolIT needed copper plates, screws, copper piping, liquid flow couplers, gap pads, and a host of other components. In modern manufacturing, none of this is made from scratch. Each component is built by someone else. The manufacturer assembles those components into the finished product. Companies like CoolIT need to establish and maintain a supply chain to provide them with the components they need. No supply chain, no manufacturing.

The company had started to establish an independent supply chain, but it wasn't yet completely operational. They were forced to continue to depend on the Shenzhen contract manufacturer, with all their known quality issues, to supply incoming product. Which meant that, as they assembled their product, they continued to run into quality problems and had to scramble to meet production commitments. Defective parts needed to be replaced, taking more time to cycle back through this shaky supply chain. Then when Cray received assemblies from CoolIT, the manufacturing team still had to install and test those cooling systems into their complete computer systems before they shipped. All the buffer Cray had in the original schedule was gone. More delay.

Peter doubled up production shifts to minimize the impact of quality-control failures as much as he could. He and Ryan, his manufacturing VP, worked the supply-chain issues, replaced suppliers where they could, and filtered out defective parts sooner. CoolIT's costs went up, and it was pretty clear that, while they were delivering, the way they were making it happen was ugly.

Executives at Cray, including Tom Hackett[28] (VP of Manufacturing), were angry. They wanted to work with a supplier who was on top of the program, not one struggling to get by. The Cray management team demanded a meeting with Peter and his team at CoolIT's headquarters in Calgary. They wanted a tour of the manufacturing plant, to make sure it really was ready. They'd been told one story. They now suspected a different reality.

> *Both quests were now approaching the **inner cave**. Peter knew CoolIT was about to face a major trial, a test of their commitment to getting past this supply-chain issue they had not resolved— not unlike John's meeting with the general at Aerospace during the Mars rover project or my meeting at Mitsubishi.*

---

28 An alias.

Peter had already figured out that he would have to add more experience to the manufacturing leadership, but he thought he was going to have more time. On this accelerated schedule, he had to build a recovery story with what he had. He, Ryan, and Pat, head of business operations, huddled to figure out what they should pitch to Cray.

"OK," Peter said. "This is going to be challenging. We need to look like we're on the ball, but we can't just say that they shouldn't worry, we've got this. We said that before and didn't deliver. What do you think, Ryan?"

"I think we need to start strong. Take them on a tour of the plant—it's up and running, just as planned." Ryan was justifiably proud of this part of the deliverable. He'd made it happen.

"OK—that sounds good. Then we need to come back to the boardroom to talk about supply chain and quality. Maybe I should lead that discussion?"

Ryan quickly agreed—that phase of the visit was going to be a lot less fun.

Peter prodded some more. "I need a color-coded breakdown for the whole supply chain—component, supplier, contract status, lead time—including planned upgrades. Green for no issues seen, yellow for mostly OK, red for those areas where we're still concerned. And I need detail on how we're handling the red cases—incoming inspection, alternate source options, whatever we might be doing. No sugarcoating problems. We have to be completely open about everything."

Peter was already thinking about the story he wanted to tell Cray and was being careful to imagine how Cray would hear it. He had to admit CoolIT's failure and describe its ideas and plans to recover, while also welcoming Cray's feedback.

Peter added, "Ryan, I really appreciate the work you have put into building up the plant. You've done a great job. But I think we can both agree you had too much on your plate to manage the supply-chain upgrade. I've started a search for an executive VP of manufacturing and supply chain to oversee both areas. That will allow you to continue focus on your core strength in manufacturing. I plan to tell Cray about this search as a part of our recovery plan."

Ryan breathed a sigh of relief. He'd wondered if he faced a much less certain future. This change was fine by him.

Toward the end of August, the Cray team flew in—leaders from manufacturing, an engineering director, and a procurement director. An intimidating turnout.

> The **ordeal**. They entered the cave, Cray to determine if they could rely on this partner, CoolIT to see if Cray was willing to continue supporting them through their struggle.

Peter had ordered the best coffee and breakfast pastries he could find. They ate and chatted for twenty minutes, then took their tour of the plant. There were a lot of questions but also nods of approval. Yes, this was real. CoolIT had delivered on this part of their promise.

They regrouped in the boardroom, a large executive office looking out onto a shopping center, beautiful blue skies, and a steady drone from airplanes flying overhead on approach to the international airport. Now the real meeting started.

Peter opened. "Tom—is there anything you or your team want to say before we present?"

"No. We'll wait to hear your story first," Tom said.

"OK. The elephant in the room is low quality in our supply chain. We promised that we would replace our current supplier with higher-quality sources. That hasn't yet happened, and for that we apologize. We have been working hard to absorb the impact of that slip ourselves to the greatest extent possible.

"I have details to share with you on current status. We want to be totally open with you. Good and bad, we won't hide anything. We broke your trust, and we want to regain it."

> *An honest story is the only path to salvation. Any competent executive will see through attempts to cover up or finesse bad news. CoolIT needed permission to continue on their sub-quest. They couldn't afford to create doubt about their motives.*

"Before we go through that, I also want to let you know that I have started a search for an executive VP responsible for manufacturing and supply-chain management. I'm hopeful we'll have someone in place quite soon. Tom, is there anything you'd like to say before we start into the detailed analysis?"

> *Peter was rebuilding confidence as the storyteller. Not only did he acknowledge that CoolIT messed up, but he was planning a structural change to make sure it never happened again. CoolIT was learning from its failure.*

Tom nodded. "Yes. I'll start by saying that we like working with you guys. You've done well by Cray in the past, and we liked how you approached this program. But you aren't the only game in town. You made two promises when we started down this path. First, that you'd set up your manufacturing plant here in Calgary, fixing cost and partly fixing quality. Insofar as you're now doing some of the assembly here, you've delivered on that promise.

"Second, I'll credit you for admitting you broke the second

promise—to have a fully operational supply chain. But confession doesn't fix the problem. I need you to explain how you're going to get back on track—quickly!"

Tom slipped in a threat. This wouldn't be a real ordeal if there wasn't a real chance of failure.

Peter said, "I understand, Tom. Let's start by having Ryan present current status."

So started a lengthy, often uncomfortable discussion on each point—explanations, questions, and debate, with Ryan and Peter taking notes as they went.

When they were done, Tom summed up for Cray: "Look, we're in this together. You screwed up, but I can see you're working hard to correct the problem. That's a start. However, we still have to deliver product and make money while you're fixing your supply-chain mess.

"The best way I can see to make this work is to integrate you into our daily operations, just like you are part of our team. You will have to provide daily updates as needed. You'll have to sit in on reviews with engineering, manufacturing, test, and procurement, prioritizing your production to their individual day-by-day needs.

"You need to integrate more closely with our engineering, so they know how they have to adapt. You need to integrate also with our test group, so they know what changes they may have to make. And you must integrate with our procurement team, to ensure your deliveries are aligned with our top customer schedules.

"It's going to be a big overhead for all of us. Tough—we've got to make it work. Are we agreed?"

Peter nodded. "We're agreed. We'll join daily calls for as long as you need. We'll provide a regular status update on our supply chain, and we'll coordinate manufacturing, test, and procurement priorities and status with your team. We'll summarize this in a daily report to make sure we catch any possible misunderstanding as soon as possible."

Tom nodded. "OK—let's make this happen. No more excuses."

> *Peter needed his hero's understanding, to give him room to complete his sub-quest, just as Gandalf needed the Fellowship's understanding that they must fight on at Helm's Deep until Gandalf could return with an army to overthrow the attackers.*

Some of those daily calls were painful, but they were essential to keeping faith. Peter himself was on every call for a while, resolving any open questions about CoolIT priorities where needed. Over time, they found a rhythm, and there were fewer open questions and fewer surprises.

> *The **road back** on the sub-quest. CoolIT brought their schedule and quality under control, delivering what they had already promised.*

By mid-October, Peter brought in Darko as his executive VP of manufacturing and supply-chain management. Darko was a seasoned manufacturing and operations executive. Within less than two months, he had all supply-chain problems resolved and manufacturing for Cray running smoothly.

Sometimes, you get a glimpse of hope amid all the gloom. Peter told me that in the midst of their firefighting, when they didn't know if they were recovering their earlier strong relationship or maybe losing ground to an unknown challenger, he went to the big conference on supercomputing, SC19, in Denver. A lot of their customers go to the show. It's a good opportunity to network and to see what the competition is doing and what might be coming next.

A part of the exhibition area was dedicated to liquid cooling, now mandatory for this class of computing. And there was Cray, demonstrating the CoolIT product in their booth and touting its abilities in their system. Peter and his team were having challenges— they were frustrated and concerned, worried they were going to be kicked out—and yet Cray was showing off their solution in the biggest supercomputer show in the world.

Peter saw Intel, Dell, and several other customers at the show, highlighting how they also used CoolIT products. That raised his spirits. In crises like these, it's easy to be overwhelmed by challenges, to lose sight of successes. SC19 reminded him that his company was doing well. Not a time to coast, certainly, but not a time to despair, either.

"By the end of the year, we had caught up." Peter couldn't help but grin. "Cray continued to order this product in high volumes going into the new year, and I'm cautiously optimistic that we've gotten over the hump."

*The **resurrection**. CoolIT had battled together with Cray through the recovery and had emerged on the other side in victory. Their plant and supply chain were fully operational, in safe hands, delivering on Cray's needs.*

I asked Peter what he felt he learned from the whole experience. He told me that he sensed that one person on his team was way overloaded, trying to take on too much. His gut told him he should bring in a senior executive. Peter was acting CEO, and he had wanted to let the incoming CEO, not yet hired, pick his own team. But he didn't have time. He had to fix a live customer problem. Darko quickly proved to be the right choice. I don't know that any of us would have made a better decision than Peter made under those circumstances.

> Peter **returned with the elixir**. It was a journey full of trials, and the cost of failure could have been catastrophic, but finally CoolIT's vision and courage were rewarded. Peter had seen Cray and others showing off the CoolIT products at the most prestigious supercomputer show in the world. The Calgary manufacturing operation was now fully functional, giving them an important advantage in these trade-challenged times and in the future. CoolIT emerged from the trial a better and stronger version of the company they had been before they accepted the challenge.
>
> Peter admits that stories like this are never truly over. They're more like a TV series—each episode opening with a new challenge to overcome, a new battle to test their resolve, ending (with luck) in victory. Then the cycle starts again in the next episode. Perhaps the hero is acquired and CoolIT will have to prove themselves again to a bigger and less forgiving hero. That's the nature of business.

TAKEAWAYS

Real growth is rarely painless. When you head into unfamiliar territory to meet a larger goal that your hero now expects of you, you're going to make mistakes. This need to start a sub-quest is common when a hero sees promise in you and your magic sword, but needs more in order to satisfy the larger quest. Then you must start your own journey within your hero's bigger journey, to meet that goal. Your journey will follow the same stages in miniature—crossing the threshold, tests, allies, enemies, the inner cave and the ordeal, and finally a reward. Like all journeys, your quest will run into setbacks and delays, testing your confidence and your hero's patience. You will need to lean on your hero's understanding from time to time to see you through.

At the same time, you should remember that you are in this position because you had the foresight and courage to accept an ambitious goal—to take risks that led you into this ordeal but which on the other side will lead to a reward and a resurrection for your hero and for you. You will both emerge stronger and more capable. You will have proven yourself a more experienced mentor and a more competitive player in your market. You will have earned an elixir that will separate you in new adventures from less ambitious and less courageous competitors.

Like all journeys, your quest will run into setbacks and delays, testing your confidence and your hero's patience. You will need to lean on your hero's understanding from time to time to see you through.

REVIEW

This story has some similarities with the Mitsubishi story—an angry customer, getting the relationship back on track—but it also has some important differences. My performance in Osaka was just that: a performance, based on a lot of work I'd done back at the factory, together with an effective if lucky performance in delivery. My task was ultimately to communicate progress with more empathy and understanding of my hero's needs than my colleagues had.

Peter had a different challenge. CoolIT needed to launch a quest within a quest, an extra level of complexity with extra challenges and ordeals, similar in structure to journeys we've seen earlier.

Growing companies also outrun their ability to meet directly with as many potential customers as they need to support continued growth. They must persuade possible customers to find them. Which brings me next to how to tell a story to all the people you can't meet face-to-face—through your marketing message. Messaging over the internet is even more relevant today as we adapt to the pandemic and life beyond the pandemic. We need to know how to tell our stories well to audiences we can't see, don't know, and can't respond to in real time. We need to market effectively, as we'll see in this next story.

CHAPTER 6

A Marketing Story

I talked to Lou Covey[29] last year, gathering background for this book. Lou told me he'd bought a Chevy Cruze recently, and he told me why he chose that car. He did a lot of research with no particular model in mind. He was more interested in looking at capabilities and reviews. Then he ran searches: analyst reviews, service reviews, mileage reviews, safety reviews, resale value, that kind of thing. He'd never heard of Chevy Cruze, but in his searches, it kept checking more of his boxes than other vehicles. Lou bought the car. Only after that did he start noticing ads for Chevy Cruzes—on billboards, on the TV, on the internet. All the money Chevy invested in direct promotion had no impact on Lou's decision

---

29   Lou is a freelance columnist at EEWeb and has lots of background in marketing through social media.

to buy. The reviews and opinion pieces did all the work. Lou was *influenced* to buy the car. Not *sold*.

Some say that, in the internet age, a buyer is already 60 percent of the way to a decision before she wants to see promotional material or a sales pitch. There's heated debate around that number, but whatever the right percentage might be, that's a huge chunk of buyer decision-making over which you as a seller have no control unless you actively work at it. Direct promotion—a shameless product plug—doesn't help, any more than it helped Chevy get Lou's business. We tune out those ads in research, unless we've already made our decision and just want to double-check. Research-worthy advice for most of us goes into promotion-free, information-rich articles, like "Do you care about safety? Here's a checklist of things you should be looking for." Those articles are sourced in journalist interviews, or more often now[30] in blogs you write yourself—short, engaging stories published online.

"OK," you think, "I've got this. The Hero's Journey. The only difference here is that the story goes into a blog. No big deal." But it is a big deal. Our readers are busy people. When they're open to a little blog browsing, they're looking for light reading, not hard work. Something topical, relevant to their needs, intriguing, and above all short, no more than 500–800 words. If you want to influence, you have to fit inside that attention span, far too short to take your reader through all the stages of a Hero's Journey. Instead you'll have to share a highlight—a teaser to get your reader curious, wanting to learn more, to click through to your website to read the full story. That's the singular purpose of a blog. Not to be an alternate telling of the whole story, but to be a movie trailer, sharing just enough detail to get a reader eager to see the full movie.

For this reason, my story in this chapter mirrors the blog con-

---

30 Unfortunately, real journalists are in short supply these days.

straint through a series of short stories, each the length of a blog. These stories still connect to the Hero's Journey, as excerpts.

* * *

I'll start with a mantra I've mentioned many times throughout this book. You as the writer are not the hero. Your reader is the hero. You are the *mentor*. Why do I keep repeating this point? Because that certainly wasn't how I started blogging. My intentions were honorable enough. I felt responsibility to deliver value for the money I was being paid for each blog. But I thought it was important to polish the image I was projecting in my readers' minds, the image of who I am. With that in mind, it seemed obvious at the time that I should present myself as a very clever person, a teacher who would naturally attract flocks of followers. Here's the opening sentence from one of my early efforts: "To fans of Gödel, Escher, and Bach (the Eternal Golden Braid), there is an appealing self-referential elegance to the idea of verifying a network switch in a cloud-like resource somewhere on the corporate network."

Wow! What a pompous ass. I can't read that now without cringing. Another post wasn't quite as ornate in phrasing but displayed just as much self-admiration in the title and theme, "Perfecting the Great Verification Fugue." I play classical piano. Michael Sanie, a friend and the VP requesting the blog, is also a classical pianist. The subject matter was quality verification for chip design, but this I thought was a better choice for a theme. The structure of fugues, a favorite of Bach, guided the blog. I was gracious enough at the end to explain the concept of a fugue, with popular examples, for the masses who probably didn't understand this style of composition.

The pompous ass strikes again.

I did more of the same, having fun with literary allusions—"Is this a dagger I see before me?" "Ask not for whom the bell tolls," "In low voltage timing, the center cannot hold," and more. I got my inspiration from reading *The Economist*, a magazine whose writers have a gift for titles like these. That magazine produces deep-dive analyses of business and political trends for subscribers wanting polished and thoroughly researched opinion pieces. Blog readers don't have time for such depth. They want a quick and useful read. I had got my plan backward. I was working hard to impress my audience, make myself the hero of these stories. I should have been designing my blogs with more thought to what my readers wanted to see.

That was a painful realization. I grew up in England, a country in which self-promotion is the worst sin imaginable. I needed to think more about what my audience wanted. They wanted to read someone writing on a topic in which the writer had proven expertise—someone reliable.[31] You can't build that trust unless you post regularly, maybe once a week on a dependable range of topics.[32] They want an easy, conversational writing style, a friend and colleague chatting with them, not a professor droning through a college lecture. Most important, they want someone who can inform them on questions important to their needs, trigger new insights, and make them look like the smartest person in the room at the next staff or board meeting.

> *You are the **mentor**, but you can't see or interact with your heroes. You have to intuit what your audience wants. You don't want to push, telling them what to do. You want to encourage; inspire them to figure out what they should do for themselves, then call them to action ... nudged on by a little guidance from you.*

---

31 My thanks to Lou for this insight. He has been blogging a lot longer than I have.

32 For anyone with a busier schedule than I have, once a month is OK too. Less frequently is not so effective.

* * *

A blog should be a teaser, a highlight taken from a more complete Hero's Journey, but from where? One obvious starting point is the *call to adventure*. Here the goal is to get your hero excited about a new opportunity or concerned about a potential threat in a rapidly changing landscape. As an example of the first type, I'll share with you a blog I wrote with CEVA, a company with a lot of experience and technology in audio, voice, and wireless applications. CEVA serves companies—their *heroes*—who build the consumer applications that need these core technologies: smart speakers, smartphones, smart just about everything. One example of a hot consumer application today where CEVA plays an important role is wireless earbuds, those tiny little speakers you stick in your ears to listen to playlists from your phone, without dangly wires getting in the way.[33] As a technology "inside," not immediately visible, CEVA wanted to grow awareness among wireless earbud makers that CEVA is an experienced *mentor* that can help them realize their plans to offer state-of-the-art products to consumers. To do that, I wanted to generate excitement about the consumer opportunity—to call these potential heroes to action by helping them realize that stasis was not an option, that they should jump on this opportunity before their competitors. And that CEVA could help them deliver that great experience.

I found an article in *The Economist* on wireless earbuds,[34] which I referenced in the blog. This set up the call to adventure—a trend that caught the attention of *The Economist* will also spark interest in the

---

33   All of these short stories are based on blogs I published in SemiWiki, under my byline.

34   "The buzz around AirPods," The Economist, December 18, 2019, https://www. economist.com/business/2019/12/18/the-buzz-around-airpods.

kind of readers CEVA would like to inspire. I continued with more market insight, gleaned from that article and others.[35] We already know that huge investment goes into monetizing visual content for our phones, tablet computers, and TVs, through content providers like Warner Media, Disney, and Netflix. There's now a push into monetizing our ears, driven by Apple, for example, on the hardware side, with Spotify and Liberty Media on the content side. The audio market isn't yet as big as the video market, but it's growing quickly. Apple's AirPods are believed to be the fastest growing of all its product lines, expected to top $15 billion in sales in 2021. Spotify and others are aggressively expanding into streaming and podcasts. This is going to be a huge opportunity for earbud makers.

How could CEVA help these heroes? First through their support for the recently upgraded Bluetooth standard, which offers higher quality at lower power in wireless earbuds, along with some amazing new possibilities. One is in improved stereo quality. The earlier standard only supported one wireless channel between the phone and the earbuds and was forced to handle stereo in a convoluted way, transmitting both left and right audio signals together to the right earbud, where they were split apart. The right channel was played on the right earbud, the left channel was forwarded to the left earbud. Earbud makers used software tricks to synchronize left and right channels, but it never sounded quite as good as hearing the music on stereo headphones, where left and right are naturally in sync. The new Bluetooth standard fixes this problem, wirelessly transmitting left and right channels separately and correctly synchronized. The standard delivers higher stereo quality, and doesn't drain the tiny batteries in those earbuds as quickly.

We wanted to build more excitement, to project what could be

---

35   *BusinessWeek, Forbes,* and other magazines of that type can be a great resource.

possible through the eyes of a consumer. With an extension to the standard called LE Audio, people can share their audio streams. Joe's listening to a great song and wants Sue to hear it too? No need to hand her an earbud; just share the stream. Or multiple friends can watch a video on a phone or tablet while each enjoying their own direct audio stream. Or imagine Joe is at a sports bar—lots of screens showing lots of games, but all silently. He sees a football game that interests him and grabs the audio stream from that game. Meantime, Sue grabs the feed from a basketball game. We can all enjoy what we want to hear, when we want to hear it. Imagine the same technology deployed in an airport departure lounge, where travelers are trying to keep up to date on messages that might affect their flight. Unlike a sports bar, announcements in airports are all full volume, overlapping and competing for their attention. Wouldn't it be nice for Sue to be able to grab an audio stream for announcements just on her flight? And tune out all those annoying loudspeakers? A platform which supports LE Audio would allow your potential partners and clients—your heroes—to build such a solution.

Now the reader of our blog, our hero, is thinking "Yeah! I want my earbud product to support all those possibilities! How do I do that?" We closed the blog with a short paragraph on a mentor who can support them on that quest. Without overselling, we introduced CEVA as a widely recognized expert in wireless and audio, an expert that has been providing Bluetooth and audio products and guidance for years. An expert that is fully current with this new standard. CEVA is a mentor worth talking to.

*The **call to adventure** builds excitement about how consumers will enjoy these wonderful new possibilities in wireless earbuds, enabled by a new Bluetooth standard. These are earbuds con-*

> sumers will want to use everywhere, while exercising and work-
> ing, certainly, but also in sports bars, at airports, who knows
> where else? And the elixir—providing a solution like this will tap
> a huge and growing market. I closed with an introduction to a
> **mentor** who could help them get there, because we didn't want
> to kill an exciting story with a commercial. We wanted to influ-
> ence, not sell.

* * *

There's a story behind my next story. I was working with Kurt Shuler, VP of Marketing at Arteris IP. Our goal was to write a *call to adventure* blog to attract companies building artificial intelligence (AI) chips— the kind of chips used to support voice control through your TV remote. We would start by calling attention to the explosive growth in this area, pointing out that all of these chip designers need on-chip networks, networks whose complexity is growing rapidly. This is a technology in which Arteris IP is expert. The call to adventure would highlight the unique demands that AI places on the on-chip network and what the network must support to meet those demands. Not so different from the last story, except that here the heroes would be chip designers rather than consumer-product designers. However, in our discussion we found a more urgent theme, shifting our focus to a new story—a story that better illustrates a call to action defined not just by an opportunity, but by an impending threat.

Arteris IP started working with Cambricon some time ago. Cambricon is a Beijing-based startup in AI chips. It took a very clever approach to its AI platform, which helped it win a design with Huawei.[36] That chip appeared in the Kirin 970 smartphone. Then Huawei decided to build its own AI chip for its next-generation phone, the Kirin 980, now in production. Cambricon is now targeting datacenter AI training applications—the kind of applications where NVIDIA has built a big presence.

In the meantime, in the realm of cloud applications, consider Baidu, effectively the Google of China. It has been working hard on AI for many of the same reasons as Google, in areas such as image search and autonomous driving. It also works closely with the Chinese government on applications such as intelligent video surveillance. Baidu started its development in AI using programmable chips. More recently, it developed its own custom AI chip, Kunlun, and it plans to continue on that path. Another startup in this area is Lynxi, also targeting an architecture for both training and inferencing in the datacenter. Kurt added that there were many more Chinese startups and big companies following similar paths. Even more interesting, he saw much more AI chip activity in China than in the US or Europe.

Wow! This is a big story: the very rapid growth of AI chip development in China, overshadowing comparable efforts in the US and Europe, at least in numbers of ventures. *A call to adventure* based on our heroes facing an imminent threat. We wrote this blog with that topic as the emphasis. We didn't even talk about technological details. But we still brought it back to the *mentor*. Arteris IP is actively working with all these companies.

> By implication (no need to say it), the **mentor** must be well
> plugged in to activity in this field. And they must have a pretty

---

36 Another Chinese company, frequently in the news these days over their dominance in 5G.

good magic sword, their technology, for all those companies to be picking it up.

*This was a good example of an influence blog. A **call to adventure** for anyone in AI tech outside China. You can imagine the tension this would build in the rest of the world. They wonder, "Are we at risk of losing this market? Is this going to be a big geopolitical problem? We'd better check with analysts, clients, suppliers, engineering staff. We need to talk to a **mentor** like Arteris IP. They seem to know what's going on."*

* * *

Another good place in the journey around which you can build interest is the *ordeal*. Your reader is already planning a journey, like Lou wanting to buy a new car. They know what they want, and they know there are hazards along this path. Maybe they're not clear about all the hazards. Or maybe they think they understand, but their understanding is incomplete and they want advice.

In another blog I wrote with Arteris IP, we wanted to attract the attention of innovators in automotive electronics, to highlight why they need to work with suppliers who are experts in safety, an area where Arteris IP is very strong. For modern cars, electronics is a booming market with huge opportunities for differentiation. This is our *call to adventure*. We want features like automatic braking if a pedestrian is detected ahead of the car. We want self-parking. We even hope for fully autonomous driving. But those features have to be safe. If your phone misbehaves, it's annoying and you reboot. When electronics in a car misbehave, people die. The ISO 26262 standard aims to minimize this possibility through a process which everyone in the supply chain must follow, from component builders to carmakers. Since the document is long and complex, not all participants have the same level of understanding. Their grasp of the document can range from "we read it, we get it" to "we've been deeply involved in this standard for years, we serve on the standard committee, we've worked with many customers on ISO 26262; this is in our DNA." Arteris IP is a supplier in the second group, a proven *mentor*. It knows that many of its competitors are in the first group, claiming expertise but clearly not mentor-level. Kurt regularly asks me to blog on the safety standard, to highlight the likely *ordeal* that prospective customer (heroes) will suffer in working with suppliers who lack a complete understanding.

He told me that a hero in the supply chain must do their own checks to *fully* qualify what they deliver. They can't just qualify what they added on top of the components they got from their providers. For full qualification, they must check and include compliance documentation sent by each one of those suppliers. Did a provider simply attach a checklist on their product, or did they follow the full process? Do they have a dedicated ISO 26262 quality team? What evidence can they offer to prove they follow the process? If these documents are not provided, the hero's own customers will demand they go back and assemble that evidence. Which creates more work and delay, adding to the ordeal. Some iteration in development will be unavoidable, but no hero wants to iterate over issues resulting from a supplier's weak understanding of the standard.

Suppliers like to prove they're following processes by showing they've adopted quality management tools. These can be useful, but they only scratch the surface. It's much more important to demonstrate ingrained practices centered on people, training, organization, and documentation. To prove an organization is following such a system, a company must prove that the system is a part of the total company culture for executives, marketing personnel, engineering staff, documentation teams, quality assurance managers, application engineers, and others. Documented evidence supports continued adherence to those practices over a significant period—the kind of evidence a true mentor has in abundance. We wanted our readers to understand that their suppliers weren't simply on the hook to deliver a product. They would need to back up their quality claims with lots of evidence of their compliance with the standard and lots of experience in where all the real pitfalls might lie—evidence and experience our heroes would be unlikely to find in a less seasoned mentor.

One more area that highlighted the importance of an experienced mentor is in something called "assumptions of use." A supplier will build a product to be used in ways they consider reasonable. But "reasonable" is a very subjective term. The standard manages that subjectivity by requiring the mentor and hero to develop an interface agreement, detailing assumptions and responsibilities for both parties. This takes a lot of thought and work on both sides and is not something a supplier can fix in a product tweak or process automation. It can only be satisfied by documentation, review, and constant checking and debate on both sides—another challenge our readers may not have considered, and another reason they want to work with a mentor who's seen it all before.

I closed with a reminder of the end goal, *returning with the elixir*. Following the process is hard work, but it doesn't have to be any more challenging than necessary. Working with the right mentor can help the hero get through the ordeal with a minimum of delay, to seize their ultimate prize—hitting the market window, capturing significant new business, and further enhancing their reputation as a supplier in this domain.

> *This is a classic **ordeal** blog. Your hero thinks they know what challenges they're going to face. But you understand those challenges in much more detail than your competitors have told them. This hero might want to consider you as their **mentor**, a mentor who has traveled this journey many times and can show them an efficient path through the ordeal, who fully understands the myriad challenges ahead, and who won't be learning on the fly, delaying the schedule and losing the hero business opportunity.*

* * *

A different type of ordeal blog acknowledges a concern the reader already has, a reason they want to remain in *stasis*. To jog them out of stasis, you can expand their perspective, to show that in a rapidly shifting landscape, they need to worry about a larger range of concerns for which remaining in stasis is in fact the riskiest choice. One blog I wrote along these lines was on a hot topic for many tech companies: balancing the security of managing their trade-secret technical computing in their own datacenters against moving it all to the cloud. I wrote this blog with Metrics, a cloud applications provider for chip designers.

We set context first with a nod to the temptation of comfortable stasis. Why move to the cloud at all? We answered that question with a *call to adventure*. In-house datacenters tie up a lot of capital and expense, and demand continues to grow. A datacenter is a money pit. Why not outsource it? In the cloud you can pay for the capacity and performance you need as you need it. Got a big surge coming next week? No problem; just buy more capacity for that week. You can be more agile and more competitive if you're not trying to manage a huge in-house capital and expense sink. Then I acknowledged the inevitable counterargument: many of your technical experts see huge risk in this change. The core value of the company is in your tech data. We're always hearing about computers in big organizations being hacked. If your precious data is stolen and used to build competing products, or to exploit weaknesses in your products, your company could go under. At least if you keep that computing internal you can watch it carefully, make it as secure as possible. Much safer not to change, they think. Just keep throwing more money at the datacenter.

We offset that one concern with much larger security concerns when staying in-house. Who is going to do a better job on security— an overworked and underpaid in-house IT organization, or leading-edge, highly paid teams in cloud businesses with tens of billions of dollars in revenue? Your in-house datacenter may be much higher risk. There's also a liability question. Tech companies work with partner data and must sign liability agreements guaranteeing "best efforts" in maintaining the security of that data. The obvious reference for "best efforts" is the openly published best practices from the cloud experts, companies who invest very heavily in security, much more than your IT team could possibly afford. However hard your IT folks might work, their efforts can never approach the best efforts of those cloud enterprises. That's the way an unbiased jury would see it.

> *In the role of mentor, we make the call to action. Stasis, hunkering down and staying safe with what you know, is an illusion. Making the leap to a new path is the only reasonable play.*

There's another legal consideration. According to standard technology-licensing agreements, a tech company's trade-secret data must be held in escrow by a third party. If your company goes under, your customers then have rights to that data to help them figure out a way to maintain their product and services without your help. Those escrow services are now moving to the cloud also. Your highly sensitive tech data is already in the cloud anyway. The genie is out of the bottle.

All of which makes sense, yet fear of the unknown is still a powerful motivator. Readers feel safest with what they already know. What evidence do you, the mentor, have that moving critical data to the cloud is secure? Readers should look at their finance department, their HR department, and their legal department. All of the financials of the company are already in the cloud: accounting, loan commitments, equity agreements, all of it. All of the HR data: payroll, insurance (bound by HIPAA[37] agreements), complete employee databases, employee agreements. All of the legal data: contracts, licensing agreements, compliance documentation. Leaking any of that information could be just as damaging to the company as leaking tech data. Our readers' fears are understandable, but true risk has to be viewed in a larger context. Our message is to the reluctant hero: "the rest of your enterprise is already confident your data is secure in the cloud because they have ample proof; everyone else is doing the same thing. The track record for security in the cloud is already proven."

> *Sometimes, to see an ordeal in the right perspective, it's help-ful for a **mentor** to raise awareness that the one obstacle your reader sees in a change is not nearly as bad as the obstacles*

---

37   A US standard which requires that personal medical data is kept confidential.

> they will face by remaining in **stasis**. And of course, that the one obstacle they imagine in the change is much less of a concern than they thought.

TAKEAWAYS

Your reader is the hero. You want to influence them, not browbeat them into your viewpoint. Expose them to intriguing new ideas, a more rounded understanding of a complex topic, a broader context for their concerns. Forget all those guidelines you learned from the marketing team. All that "leading provider" and "best-in-class" boilerplate—anything that looks like hype. Ditch the product promotion. That stuff doesn't influence; it makes us suspicious. Save promotion for your website. Talk the way you would to a friend. Win their trust. Blog readers never trust anyone who is blatantly selling. That's a serious problem in influencing; once lost, trust is very hard to regain.

But once trust is gained, you have a powerful advantage. Your reader, your hero, also reads to be informed. To stay on a par with or—better yet—ahead of peers in knowing what's happening in the industry. Because peers, managers, customers, and investors notice who is plugged in to current views and trends. Once you have built trust, your insight provides your hero with that personal advantage, further reinforcing trust—a virtuous cycle.

Write your blog as a teaser to the main story. Your single-minded goal is to capture the reader's attention and get them interested enough to want to learn more. You can't do that if your blog is a spoiler for the main story, or if it looks like you've covered everything important. You have to leave them wanting more.

The call to adventure is a good teaser. Tempt your reader with what they will see as opportunity—a new and exciting market with a sense of the elixir at the end of the journey. Show them how you can help them expand business opportunities and differentiate themselves from competitors. Or help them see and better understand emerging threats. In either case, gently encourage them to seek you out as a mentor to help them reach for these opportunities or understand the challenges they will face.

The ordeal is another good teaser. Here you're talking to a reader who is already committed to, or maybe opposing a new direction. They want to know what problems they're going to run into. You can enumerate those problems with just enough detail for them to see your experience. Or, as in one example I shared, you can help them put those challenges in perspective. Again, hint that you are the kind of mentor they need, a mentor willing to share the facts, not shower them in happy talk.

REVIEW

There's a lot more to marketing than blogging—white papers, case studies, websites, webinars, conferences, keynotes, all directed toward building a brand and building leads. I've chosen to feature blogging here, not only because of my experience in this area, but because it reflects an important trend away from direct product promotion toward more emphasis on influence marketing, especially through telling the reader stories.

Stories, and elements of the Hero's Journey in particular, are important not only in first capturing the interest of a prospective customer but also in keeping that interest when she wants to dig deeper. If she saw the trailer, was excited, and wanted to see the movie, imagine how disappointed she would be if she clicked through a link and ran straight into a hard sell. What happened to the movie? The material on the other end of the link should expand on the trailer, tell the whole story. Once your role as an expert and mentor is established, then your reader may be ready to learn more about how your products can help.

Boosting sales will power a business along its journey, but there's no more exciting story in the life of any venture than the exit story—when you're acquired by another enterprise, or by a private equity firm, or you make it onto a public market. That's the end goal that many of us dream of—our path to riches. An exit story is the topic of my next chapter.

CHAPTER 7

An Exit Story

We all want to make the world a better place. We'd also like to be rewarded for our efforts, perhaps by being acquired. We've built a great product, and we see a huge opportunity. We just have to pick the lucky suitor who'll get to take us home. If only it were that simple. My friend Bert Clement[38] shared a cautionary tale with me. When he was at Verisign, they bought a number of companies. Some worked out, but not all. In one, there was fantastic synergy between the businesses, and the acquisition started with great revenues and profitability. But most of the execs from the acquired company left, and the business stopped performing. The investment turned into

---

38   At that time CFO and COO of Atrenta, the company I cofounded, now CEO of Retail Solutions.

a dud. Experienced buyers have suffered from these kinds of deals before, or they know others who have. When they're thinking about a deal, they don't have the benefit of our rose-colored glasses; they're thinking about the ways the marriage could backfire.[39] Helping your investor-hero perceive a happy balance between opportunity and risk takes great skill in influencing.

That mixture of excited anticipation and cautious skepticism makes for a lot of dramatic tension, further heightened when there's more than one bidder. As a potential acquiree, you plan the way you'd like the story to unfold, but the closer you get to the climax, the more it develops a life of its own. The same could be said for exit stories. Again, a nod to Stephen King ... we hold the pen, but the story inevitably writes itself, and we have to go with the flow. You can exercise some control over the story, but don't kid yourself that you can plan out every detail of how your corporate courtship will unfold. Like a good writer, you need to stay nimble.

I have chosen a story about the exit I know best, for a company called Atrenta. This was the company Ajoy Bose and I started some twenty years ago. Ajoy, the hero of this story, was our Chairman, President, and CEO. You'll see just how spot-on Stephen King's guidance is in this story.

I'm breaking with my rule here that the hero should be the customer (the buyer in this case) and the seller should be the mentor.[40] Since everything about the buyers must be held secret, I've made Ajoy the hero of our story. However, you should

---

39 The great majority of acquisitions fail. See, for example, Axial's "9 Reasons Acquisitions Fail—and How to Beat the Odds," https://www.axial.net/forum/9-reasons-acquisitions-fail-beat-odds/.

40 These deals are bound up in a lot of legal paperwork, especially nondisclosure agreements. In deference to those agreements (to which I am also bound), I have anonymized certain names, and I have been careful to avoid sensitive details.

> *remember that your potential buyer is your hero. You are not the hero, even though you may be strongly tempted to believe you are!*

* * *

This tale started with a product we called SpyGlass. SpyGlass checks that a chip design complies with well-established best practices for design and implementation. At the time that we built SpyGlass, the only similar product had been acquired into, then disappeared inside a larger company. I believed that hole in the market needed to be plugged. SpyGlass was our answer to that need.

Most design software vendors thought this kind of product, commonly called a linter, was too niche and too low value to be worth a lot of attention. That view was amply justified by the very low revenues that earlier ventures of this kind had generated—no more than a few million dollars. Who wanted to waste time on that kind of product when there were billion-dollar markets to chase?

That was fine by Atrenta. We were able to build a market and a reputation against indifferent competition. By the time the company started looking seriously at an exit, our revenues were approaching $50 million per year, our year-over-year growth was in double digits, we dominated our market, and the SpyGlass brand was recognized worldwide. Not bad for a linter.

The general market in which Atrenta operated is known as electronic design automation (EDA). This market is quite small by most standards today, maybe around $9 billion in 2020, though it is essential for the design of every electronic device. A half-trillion-dollar semiconductor industry depends on these tools, and e-commerce ($25 trillion) and mobile devices ($4 trillion) in turn depend on semiconductors. EDA is pivotal to what we all understand as the modern age.

> We were in **stasis**. We had a nice successful business in a strong position in one part of EDA. We were growing, having fun.
>
> A side note. I was deeply involved in the company in many ways, but I was not directly involved in the exit. To avoid confusion in the rest of the story, I'll tell the story from this point on as an observer, not a participant.

That said, Atrenta had been underway since the early 2000s, surviving two major downturns: the dot-com crash and the Great Recession. Along the way, Atrenta had picked up a couple of investment rounds. The investors wanted to know when they would be able to cash out. A reasonable question, but Atrenta was not going to be a cheap date.

> They were **called to adventure**, pushed to move out of their comfortable reality, looking for companies who might acquire them.

This industry is dominated by a few big players—the kind of companies that might be likely to buy Atrenta. Five years after the company was founded, one of those companies approached Ajoy, interested in what it might take to do a deal. That courtship fizzled fast. The prospective buyer realized there was a big gap between what they wanted to pay and what the Atrenta board and investors expected. In 2008, the Great Recession hit. Markets were spooked and exits of any kind were put on hold. Atrenta had to put its dreams on the shelf and just focus on getting by.

*They were **refused**. Some buyers prefer cheap acquisitions. That's their standard approach to deals. Which can be OK if you built your business without investment funding. That wasn't an option for Atrenta. They returned to stasis, waiting for a better climate for acquisitions.*

Two or three years later, Fed[41] stimulus plans were paying off and markets warmed up again. Consumers and businesses were buying more electronics, and semiconductor companies were building more chips to drive those electronics. EDA companies rediscovered robust growth and were back on the lookout for any competitive advantage they might find through acquisitions.

Ajoy talked regularly with Mike Hackworth, a board member from the early days of the company and a trusted advisor. They'd often meet for breakfast at the Southern Kitchen in Los Gatos, a classic American breakfast and lunch joint. At one of these breakfasts, early in 2012, Ajoy asked Mike what suggestions he had to stir up acquisition interest. Mike told him that the first thing to understand is that companies aren't sold, they're bought. Ajoy should invest time in influencing potential buyers, not pitching the company for sale.

*Mike was Ajoy's **mentor**. He promoted the importance of influencing, the same technique we examined in Chapter 6. Mike suggested that influencing is just as important with buyers as it is with customers.[42]*

After his discussion with Mike, Ajoy started his influencing campaign. He'd meet regularly with executives at each of a handful

---

41 The Federal Reserve, the US central bank.

42 Sadly, Mike passed away later in the year. We can't always keep our most influential mentors.

of companies. Not to ask them to buy Atrenta, just to provide them with an update: the latest on the company, a general sense of growth rate, some important recent deals, what drove those customers to buy, where they were headed next. Naturally, those executives knew why Ajoy was giving them these updates, but they were happy to listen. These were no-pressure discussions, keeping them informed but with no expectations.

> *Influencing in an exit is not so different from influencing through blogging. You don't need a full journey. You should share excerpts from the journey, especially the call to adventure to highlight the opportunity and your possession of the elixir to highlight your proven success.*
>
> *In starting his influencing, Ajoy had **crossed the threshold**. He was setting an implicit expectation that Atrenta was in play, looking for a buyer. There was no good way to turn back from that point.*

Ajoy told me that through this period, our big semiconductor customers were suggesting to their major EDA vendors, "You should buy Atrenta. They have good technology. If you acquire them, we would probably buy more." All providing further influencing nudges, which was very encouraging, but not really leading anywhere. He wanted to trigger a bit more action. In 2013, he got together with Bert. "You've been through a couple of acquisitions," Ajoy said. "How can I ramp up the story I'm telling potential bidders?"

Ajoy and Bert were a well-matched team: Ajoy was the acknowledged leader, ambitious in his vision for what the company could achieve, meticulous in attention to detail, always concerned for the best interests of all his team. Bert was the no-nonsense finance guy, connecting that vision and concern to the ground reality. He'd been round the acquisition track a few times and knew the hard truths.

*Bert was an **ally** and a **mentor**.*

Bert didn't hesitate. "Three things. First, we need to share more detail; we should give them our standard pitch, show them how we sell to our customers. And we need to beef up the customer logo slide. For this pitch we need all the logos, not just the usual set.[43]

"Second, our marketing team should do an analysis on our growth potential. For each major account, how much business have we exploited so far and how much more real opportunity could be uncovered if we pulled out all the stops? I want to show we're just at the start of our growth."

Atrenta had an experienced marketing exec who'd led marketing in a few ventures and knew how to separate sales hope from reality, and how to see opportunities that sales might not see. He knew how to develop a good view of all Atrenta's major engagements—what deals and what growth were possible in each.

"Third, we need to show them some key financial metrics. I'm not talking about full financial statements and revenue projections. Just three numbers: revenue, gross margin (an indication of profitability), and revenue growth rate. Our revenue looks good, but we need to work on margin and growth."

They wanted to share evidence that the company already had the elixir; that they were valuable to buyers because they had assets those buyers could not easily acquire on their own; that Atrenta had built a successful, profitable business with healthy growth and a loyal customer base.

---

43 Companies like to list customer logos—"See all these great companies that are already working with us!" But some customers, often the ones you'd really like to list, forbid you from publicizing the relationship.

Bert continued, "For margin, you need to clamp down on expenses. Show that you're running a tight ship. I don't think that will be too difficult.

"Revenue growth is going to be harder, but I have an idea. I suggest that I take over sales. I'll make it much more aggressive— bigger commissions for good deals. And I'm going to close more deals. That will put a lot of pressure on the support team and R&D, which will force the organization to become more efficient, move us onto a steeper growth curve."

Bert had laid down the gauntlet. They couldn't continue with business as usual if they wanted to get serious about becoming an attractive buyout target. Sales needed to rise, efficiencies had to be put in place, challenges should be faced. Stasis was no longer an option. Were they ready to leap? Ajoy, our hero, who had been flirting with buyers in diners, safe, now responded to The Call.

"I'll make it happen," said Ajoy.

These changes were tough at first. Sales managers weren't convinced it would work; some even quit. Engineers struggled to manage handholding customers through a higher volume of deals. Everyone was shocked that the days of anything-goes expense reports came to a screeching halt, and they all had to get their expenses current.[44] Fairly quickly, though, Ajoy and Bert started to see turn-around in those key financial metrics.

*Our hero faced **tests**, challenges, resistance.*

---

44   Some had unclaimed expenses dating back a year or more.

Next, they had to figure out what type of deal they wanted. Ajoy pulled together a slightly larger team and asked, "Bert, why don't you walk us through the alternatives?"

Bert said, "A traditional option has always been an IPO. Back in the early 2000s, you could consider an IPO if you had around $20 million in annual revenue. But the recession hit, stricter accounting standards kicked in, and investors became fascinated with unicorns.[45] Now it's really tough to even think about an IPO until you can show $150–200 million in revenue."

He added, "There's another problem. An IPO is just the start of the path for a public enterprise. There'll be a lockup period in which we common stockholders can't sell equity. If something goes wrong, everyone else on the open market can sell their shares immediately while we have to sit on our hands and watch the value of our equity plummet.

"We also have to show the IPO investors that we're just at the start of our serious growth. The money they'll invest will propel us into much higher growth. We'll be competing with other newly public ventures, who are also claiming very exciting growth potential. We have to be just as good. We'll also be battling more seasoned competitors in our own market, reporting to a public board, generating 10-K reports and holding quarterly analysts' meetings. Just getting ready for the IPO, we'll have to hire a lot more people than we have now to manage compliance to public company requirements."

Ajoy grimaced. "Well, aside from all the hard work and risk and added staff, we're not even in the right revenue range. What else have you got?"

Bert said, "Another option, not often considered, is private equity (PE). These guys are financial investors. They might buy a

---

45   Startups with $1 billion+ valuations, like Uber, Airbnb, and Spotify.

company, generally much bigger than us, squeeze out cost, and even-tually make their money in an IPO. Sometimes they'll consolidate multiple companies together into a single entity with larger value, then float that company on the market. I don't think either will work for us. Valuations in our market are probably too small to interest PE investors.

"The most realistic option, I think, is acquisition by a strategic buyer—an M&A deal with a bigger company already in a very similar business."

"OK," said Ajoy. "Now we're back in familiar territory. There's a limited number of potential buyers, we all know that. The big EDA companies, maybe one or two others in adjacent businesses like product lifecycle management[46] (PLM), perhaps interested in expanding to support semiconductor design. Is everyone OK if we stick to this path, the strategic buyers?"

> In acquisition, "go with what you know" is always going to be the easiest path. Your story is going to run into plenty of problems anyway. No need to make them worse by heading down an unknown path.

They all agreed. Ajoy continued, "I've been staying in touch with execs at all these companies through my influencing campaign, just keeping them abreast of where we are. I can continue that, but now I want to bring you along, Bert, if I sense a nibble. Which we should now start to see, given these improved financial metrics."

> Challenges had been met and hard changes made to position

---

46 Popular in industries such as automotive and aerospace where products must be tracked from design to manufacture, release, and post-release support, through end-of-life.

> *the company more favorably for suitors. Now Ajoy and Bert approached the **inner cave.***

One of those meetings led to a discussion with FredCorp.[47] They seemed serious, but in this market, buyers knew that sellers have limited options. They'd make a very low offer, knowing that they could just wait this company out. That was what happened here. Ajoy and Bert weren't interested but agreed to stay in touch.

They built a story for another company, JoeCorp, on how Atrenta could help them in automotive electronics businesses. This story had to be a bit more elaborate—not just about what Atrenta was doing but also how they could help JoeCorp grow in a new direction, into semiconductor design support. The JoeCorp marketing people were eager—they wanted to be able to expand into new markets. The JoeCorp technical people were less enthusiastic. They didn't know anything about needs in the semiconductor business. They didn't know how to determine if Atrenta was a good fit for that objective.

> *The **ordeal** had started. Here the story was starting to develop a life of its own. No outright rejections, but no urgency to move forward, either. Some casual dates, but no one wanted to get serious.*

Ajoy knew that Deutsche Bank had recently brokered a deal for another company in our space. He signed them on to be Atrenta's banker because they had done work with BillCorp, which was also a possible buyer for the company. He also talked to his friends at TedCorp, letting them know Atrenta was in play. TedCorp told him, "We need to talk."

---

47   All company names are fictional.

This was the state of play in 2014. FredCorp might still have been possible if they knew they weren't the only bidder, but they were still digesting another recent acquisition. They just weren't ready to talk. JoeCorp, BillCorp, and TedCorp were all contenders. BillCorp and TedCorp were very active; JoeCorp was moving more slowly.

> *Two serious suitors—the story was building momentum. I asked Ajoy what triggered that momentum. He said word got around somehow—maybe Deutsche Bank, maybe leaks from any one of the companies involved, or analysts; who could tell? What was clear was that the big players knew Atrenta was getting serious attention. Everyone realized the clock had started. This story was headed to a climax, for better or worse.*

Trial valuations were floated. Here, Ajoy ran into an unexpected buyer's trick. They'd send in their sales team, tasked with creating a revenue projection for the next several years. That team would always come back with a low projection, because they knew if the deal went through, they were going to be held accountable to generate those revenues.

If you, the seller, are already generating, say, $10 million a year, the buyer's sales team might say, "The first year we'll do $5 million, because we don't know how to sell this. Over several years we'll build that up to $10 million," which justifies a ridiculously low valuation. Ajoy and Bert found out later these weren't serious numbers. Maybe some buyers hope you'll grab for it anyway, but they won't be surprised if you counter with a much higher number.

> *Another **ordeal**. Ajoy didn't know if these were serious numbers. Deal-killing numbers. Until he learned about the trick. Our hero was learning, growing.*

Ajoy called together his execs to discuss what they thought should be the valuation. He also brought in Deutsche Bank and some trusted outside advisors. Ajoy was peeved. "Now that we know these Mickey Mouse valuations aren't serious, we have to come up with our own number. Let's start with the Deutsche Bank view."

Deutsche Bank said, "In this industry, value is generally going to be a multiple of revenue. Given your revenue and the standard multiples we have seen, I think you should propose $X million."[48] Bert and the advisors agreed.

> Another invaluable **mentor**. Most ventures with serious revenue and hoping to be acquired bring in a banker to advise on pricing and to help manage the complexity of the transaction. The banker is an ally who brings knowledge, experience, and technical capacity that the hero needs to face this test.

Ajoy said, "OK, that seems fair. Now what do we think of the pros and cons of these two companies as buyers?"

The marketing head jumped in. "Both BillCorp and TedCorp would work; good market overlaps with what we do. TedCorp has a stronger overlap, though. BillCorp would be more of a departure for many of us, though it would be a chance to grow. And we all know people at both companies, probably a lot more at TedCorp."

Ajoy added, "Another consideration is culture. TedCorp is very similar in many ways to us and has the same culture as ours. A lot of BillCorp's products and customers are in different applications, and the culture is quite different."[49]

---

48 One of the most secret secrets in these deals is the price.

49 You probably wonder in what ways the cultures were different. Sorry, but this is another area where NDAs require me to let your own imagination fill in the blanks.

> *The story continued to evolve. Now that they had real numbers in mind, they were looking beyond the numbers. Most employees would make only a little from the sale, maybe nothing. They'd be working for a different company, different people, and different benefits, in a different location. Remember the Verisign story: if unhappy employees go elsewhere, the buyer could be left with a potentially crippled business. The story needed to have a good ending for **everyone**.*

Bert summarized. "Here's what I'm hearing. All things being equal, you guys would prefer TedCorp. However, if BillCorp was to tweak their number a little, you might be open to listen. Do I have that right?"

They all agreed and finalized proposals. Ajoy passed these on to his BillCorp and TedCorp contacts.

> *Too early to cry "victory." It's always good to have at least two bidders. That creates competition. But not so fast—bidders have a say, too.*

When BillCorp got the proposal, they talked to their advisors and decided to play hardball—try to push Ajoy to a lower price.

> *The **ordeal** continued. Our hero and his allies continued to fight together, to stay committed to their plan.*

Meantime, the CEO of TedCorp, driving to a board meeting, called Ajoy. He said, "I know what number you guys are expecting. Tell me a little bit more about other things in your roadmap. I'm about to present this to our board. I'll recommend we pay what you want, and I want to close the deal with some excitement about your future ideas." Ajoy suggested a couple of new directions he'd discussed internally with the Atrenta team.

Shortly afterward, Ajoy heard that TedCorp's board had agreed to his number. BillCorp was still dragging its feet.

> *A **reward**. Atrenta now had a solid offer. A very acceptable offer.*

TedCorp had figured out there was another bidder, so they wanted to wrap up the deal quickly. They asked Atrenta to sign a no-shop agreement. This agreement required that, for a period of sixty days, Atrenta could not talk to other prospective acquirers. That window would allow TedCorp to complete their due diligence, checking that everything about Atrenta was solid before finalizing the merger. TedCorp got the agreement to Ajoy within a few days.

> *The offer is just the start of the process. Due diligence is where the buyer gets to find out if everything you've been telling them is true, if all your books are in order, if there are any skeletons in the closet. The deal is finalized only when all of those steps have been completed.*

Around this time, Ajoy's mother passed away and he had to fly to India. He hadn't yet signed the agreement from TedCorp, so he called the CEO of BillCorp and told him he was now looking at a no-shop proposal from another bidder, which he would have to sign in a day or two. Did BillCorp want to reconsider its position before he signed?

Nothing concrete came back from BillCorp, so Ajoy signed the no-shop. This was on June 7, 2015. Right after signing, Atrenta and TedCorp posted a joint press release announcing TedCorp's provisional intent to acquire Atrenta. The following day, Ajoy's daughter had a C-section back in California. Ajoy had to be there, so he missed out on the fun. *Intent to acquire* press releases always generate excitement around the industry, followed by calls of congratulations, like your first baby was born or you just won the lottery. Everyone is imagining that this might happen to them, too, someday!

> The final challenges: no time for the hero and his allies to take their eyes off the ball.

When the press release went out, BillCorp suddenly woke up. The advice they had been given on playing hardball had backfired. They tried to swarm Atrenta—e-mails, voicemails, people in the Atrenta lobby; CEO, execs, personal friends at BillCorp and mutual friends at other companies all trying to get to Ajoy or anyone in Atrenta.

> The suitors had a story too. BillCorp was realizing it had over-played its hand and was now out of the running.

But a no-shop agreement is quite clear. Once signed, any discussion with other potential acquirers is forbidden during the period of the agreement. Ajoy refused to engage with BillCorp, and everyone else on his team was under the same orders. BillCorp never got to talk to them until after the deal was done.

Then the TedCorp due diligence started. A hundred people—facilities people, HR, finance, legal—all swarmed over Atrenta, checking contracts, customer agreements, warranties, whatever Atrenta had committed. It was a well-structured operation, like a machine. Within a month, due diligence was completed, and the merger agreement was signed.

> ***Resurrection.*** *The story found a happy ending. Inevitable? That's less clear. Deals like this can fall through for a million reasons—a change of heart, new priorities, acts of God. This one didn't. Atrenta and TedCorp guided it as best they could; the rest was up to fate. Finally, the hero and his allies could lay down their swords and celebrate a successful outcome.*

After the signing, the TedCorp CEO almost immediately came over to the Atrenta offices to meet the team. He gave a pitch on the history of TedCorp—how it had been very successful with mergers like this and how people acquired in those mergers had gone on to senior roles in the company. He brought along his HR people to talk about benefits and packages. It was all very professional. Ajoy told me this sealed the deal for the Atrenta people. They were going to be treated well.

> ***Return with the elixir.*** *The TedCorp CEO knew the importance of a smooth finish to the story, reassuring the Atrenta team. TedCorp smothered our folks with love and, to the best of my knowledge, five years later most of the Atrenta people are still on the team.*

Finally, since this is now public knowledge, I can tell you that TedCorp is Synopsys.

TAKEAWAYS

An M&A deal is about more than a technology/product and a price. It's also about risk. The risk that the deal could go sour. The risk that a competitor might steal you away. Creating the best impression among potential buyers is not about direct selling but telling an influencing story—perhaps with the buyers, perhaps with customers important to the buyers. That you're a hot catch, that you're organized, and that maybe they're not the only company that has noticed.

Creating the best impression among potential buyers is not about direct selling but telling an influencing story.

Careful planning is very important. If you have a hot technology, validated by a few important customers, your suitors will be chasing you for that technology. Atrenta was offering something different: market dominance in a proven product domain, plus significant revenues. It's easier to influence with a revenue story. Revenue for the acquirer will increase by a known amount, which connects directly to financial value. Influence with technology is more speculative. I'm not going to presume to offer advice in this area, since I've never gone through a technology sale. I think influencing your most important customers would be the best place to start. Their opinion may carry a lot more weight with likely buyers than your opinion.

Bert told me that in influencing, it's important to see a deal through a buyer's eyes. See them as the heroes of the story, with you as the mentor, just as in the other stories I've shared. They may see opportunity in how you can help them grow their business or may be motivated by fear of a competitor snatching you away … or both. That can only be a threat if there's more than one potential buyer. Finding multiple bidders contributes significantly to influence. There's no more powerful influencer than the fear of missing out. We have the same concerns when we make an offer on a house in a competitive market. Do they already have offers? Should we bid higher, should we improve our terms? Do we need to close quickly before another bidder beats us to it?

Experienced mentors—people and organizations who have been through acquisitions or IPOs—are incredibly important. Mike Hackworth provided invaluable guidance early on. Bert was a mentor as well as an ally, thanks to his experience at Verisign. And Deutsche Bank had experience in realistic pricing expectations. Peter Calverley from our Chapter 5 story suggested a tip for novice acquirees. The biggest problem he sees in entrepreneurs during deal discussions is overoptimism. Peter has seen good startups walk away from reasonable offers and ultimately fail, all because the offer didn't match their lottery-win expectations and they didn't have a good mentor to set them straight.

Just as important, the story must be designed to end well for everyone in the acquired company.[50] Remember that the acquisition will not be successful if key people leave: key engineering staff, key marketing staff, key technical support staff. In a technology company, these people are just as important an asset as the technology itself. They must believe they will be looked after in the new company. They won't lose their jobs or be required to move. They can continue to work with their friends and their management team. Opportunity to expand their careers will be at least as good, if not better. The story should be sensitive to their concerns, to make sure everyone feels part of an exciting future.

REVIEW

The story that goes with an exit journey will be one of the most exciting you can experience—a chance to move up to a different

---

50 Or almost everyone. Some functions are routinely cut in an acquisition, especially the sales team (not the application engineers) and general and administrative functions: finance, human resources, and IT.

lifestyle if it all works out. At the same time, exit stories are high risk. You're talking about serious money, and with serious money come serious expectations. It's a very real possibility that there are other, better ways a buyer could spend that money. They're open to hearing an exciting story about how your company might contribute to growing their story, if you can tell that story. But keep it real. These are smart and experienced people. They are not easily fooled.

When we're building a story for an exit, for any business objective, for almost any opportunity or challenge in our daily lives, we're constantly telling ourselves stories. That's how we instinctively prepare for those events and how we rationalize the outcome and maybe grow from the experience. My last story is on that topic: the stories we tell ourselves, the foundation we're constantly creating and replaying through our daily lives.

CHAPTER 8

The Stories We Tell Ourselves

You probably remember the old joke about the two shoe salesmen dispatched to a third-world country to find new markets. One sends back a message, "Situation hopeless. Nobody here wears shoes." The other salesman reports, "Fantastic opportunity! They don't have any shoes yet!" We frame opportunity or setbacks in the way we choose to see them. In storytelling terms, we first tell ourselves a story of how the world is, then we tell others that story. Our perceived

In storytelling terms, we first tell ourselves a story of how the world is, then we tell others that story. Our perceived reality becomes the "real" story we project to our audience.

reality becomes the "real" story we project to our audience.

Throughout this book I've been telling you stories about how we can communicate through stories in business life—in startups, investment, growth, marketing, and exits. Humility is central to each story. The goals of the audience are primary; our goals are secondary. We are experts in what we do, and we're right to be proud of our expertise. But successful business communication is always rooted in telling stories about our audience's goals and suggesting how we might be able to help—fitting our capabilities to their needs, not the other way around.

In this final chapter, I want to turn the focus back onto you. We're all faced with a never-ending series of situations we must decode and process, in business and in life in general. We must determine, as the "main characters" of our own lives, how we will respond to each of those events.

Say you want to meet an important executive, Heather, for a big request—a pitch to her team, asking for advice, maybe closing a deal. You get on her calendar. Then you start to tell yourself stories. That last meeting didn't go so well. Perhaps she doesn't really like you or doesn't view you as important. Maybe she doesn't have time for this meeting. What if she doesn't like your pitch? What if this meeting further undermines her view of you? Maybe you should cancel; maybe you should talk to someone else. By the time you've told yourself a story of woe, from every possible angle, you're thoroughly demoralized. Walking into the meeting, you're perspiring and nervous, hoping for a quick exit. Heather obliges.

Suppose instead you go into the meeting with this narrative. You have a clear goal in mind. Because Heather doesn't have time to just chat, she needs to know this discussion has a purpose. What does she want to hear? That you have a prepared agenda. You want to check first that this is aligned with her expectations for this meeting, and you tell her you're happy to adjust as needed to cover what she wants to hear. Perhaps she first wants to talk about her company's larger goal. Perfect! You take detailed notes. Then you'll walk efficiently through the agenda, on each point checking in with her to get feedback. Finally, you'll sum up with your key discoveries and your action items from this meeting. As you leave the room, Heather thinks, "I wish I had more people like that on my team. People who listen and respond to a client's goals, who aren't always pushing their objectives. People who understand their client is the hero."[51]

The Hero's Journey can be a useful guide to framing not only the stories we tell others, but the stories we tell ourselves, regulating our confidence, our choices, and our perspective. Situating yourself as the author of your life stories helps you recognize and prepare better for important transitions in your life, prepare more effectively for challenging conversations, and better understand the world through the eyes of your spouse, friends, or business colleagues. Viewing our lives as unfolding stories helps us both appreciate the power of our own journey and respect the time others are giving to us. Because the better we listen to and focus on the goals of the people close to us, in life and in business, the more they will be ready to listen to us. We'll learn to better respect ourselves, to grow through difficulties. My last story is on this theme: the story of how I wrote this book. A story in which I was challenged many times, sometimes by what seemed impossible hurdles. I completed my journey and, along the way, learned some important lessons.

* * *

---

51 Many sales professionals will recognize this as a standard sales skill. But it's really a life skill.

I've written a couple of books before, both self-published through SemiWiki. The only critical review these had was my own, my coauthors', and a little marketing oversight. I'd like to say I'm my own worst critic, but I'm not. A techie writing a book for techies is not much of a stretch, and I had no one leaning over my shoulder, pushing me as an author. I wanted to write my own book under just my name, no shared authorship. I wanted to be challenged by a professional reviewer. I wanted it to be a "real" book, under the imprint of a mainstream publisher. This book was on my bucket list, a legacy. I was going to share with the world my acquired wisdom on how to tell a compelling story. It would be built around a concept of three slides—the only three slides you'll ever need to create. Catchy, I thought. A shiny idea that should attract a decent number of readers, out of curiosity alone.

OK—good concept, but how was I going to get to a mainstream publisher? Everything I've read about this step demands months of isolated toil: to complete my manuscript, shop it around to publishers, sit back and wait for rejection slips. That didn't sound like a lot of fun. Sometimes luck intervenes—I was caught up in a Forbes trawl for budding authors. I didn't know how this worked, so we fumbled through some confusion about what the next steps should be, until I was kicked up to a VP who told me they were generally OK with my big-picture idea, but he wanted to know if I was serious. Did I really want to do this, or should I stop wasting their time?

*At this point, I was in **stasis**. I wanted to write this book, but I didn't yet have confirmation that any of this would be real. Maybe it was just a fantasy. Could I do this?*

At last, a no-nonsense executive. I assured him I was very serious.

I signed a first-round agreement, then started on a path to develop the general structure of the book. As input, I sent him my clever idea, an even more clever preface I had drafted, and my outline. We had another discussion; he read my outline, was very complimentary, and promptly proposed a completely different one. Oh, well. I wanted to play in the big leagues, and here I am: this is the serious feedback I've been looking for. We debated more details—what I wanted, what Forbes expected—after which I signed a publishing agreement. Finally, I was on a path to develop a real book through a real publisher!

> *I crossed the threshold. I had committed to a contract. I couldn't back out.*

At this point I was in love with my three-slide idea. #1: A big problem begging to be addressed. #2: Why what you have to offer is the best possible answer to that need. #3: Customer adoption and endorsements to prove that you have a world-beating solution. If you can't explain each point in a single slide, you haven't figured out your story yet. The publisher wanted me to explain my concept through the progression of an enterprise, from startup to exit. And since the point of the book was to explain how to tell a story, I should explain using stories. I wasn't completely sure how I would adapt to this requirement, but it didn't seem like a big hurdle. I could describe the application of the technique in different phases of the company life cycle, and I could use little stories to illustrate various key points, answering the need for stories. I knew how to do this.

The VP introduced me to my writing coach, David Allen. One of my biggest concerns in taking on this book was serious independent review. Not the "marketing markup" kind of review—redlines through my text. I wanted review of the logic and flow, pointers to improve my writing skill. David explained that his coaching would be critical review, much like what professional writers do in writing circles, providing some feedback on how I write but much more on my ability to tell my story well. This sounded fantastic—feedback to make me a better writer.

I explained my ideas and David listened carefully (and with great patience, I suspect). He told me that I had a very interesting idea, but he suggested that I could get it across and engage my reader best by telling stories. He explained the general idea—very close to the structure I've used through this book—and he pointed me to several references. I've mentioned the Stephen King book already. That one was an instant hit for me—two others not so much, though they may appeal to others.[52]

> I met my **mentor**—someone who knew much more about writing books than I did. But he wasn't going to write the book for me. David saw that I had a good set of stories to work from and some native writing ability. As my mentor, he wanted to help me draw out and build on my own abilities. In a parallel to The Lord of the Rings, David was Gandalf, I was Frodo. Gandalf's role is not to carry the ring to Mount Doom. He was a key player in the quest, but this was not his quest. As a mentor, he understood that his role was to support Frodo and to help him have confidence in his own abilities, fight through the inevitable trials, and return home with the elixir.

The story structure suggestion was a much bigger change than I had expected, but I was intrigued. I had been thinking that stories

---

52 *Bird by Bird*, by Anne Lamott—very good book, just not very relatable for me. Also, *Punching Babies*, by Adron Smitley—a quite different approach, more a build-a-book formula that didn't appeal to me.

would be decoration on my main theme. Now I started to imagine stories being the main theme. That was exciting. I started to picture a book much bigger in concept than my original idea.

There was one small problem. In preparation for this book, I'd recorded multiple interviews with friends and colleagues who had agreed to share their views on storytelling. I went into these interviews encouraging and expecting lists of things you should and shouldn't do. That's what I got. Lots of lists and no stories. Great for my original plan, terrible for my new plan. Now I had to go back and ask for stories, which was uncomfortable. I imagined them asking why I hadn't known what I wanted the first time round. Most of my interviewees were gracious enough to indulge me, not just once but in several following discussions, though I'm pretty sure I outlasted my welcome with some. However, I managed to gather enough material to visualize most of the stories that would become the heart of each chapter.

I dove into writing my first three chapters, now bubbling with inspiration. I was having a ball ... until David reviewed what I'd written and provided feedback. We would talk, he would provide coaching advice. And every round of advice seemed to hint that I wasn't rising to what he thought I could do. OK, I'd think, this time I get what my coach is telling me; I'll rewrite, we'll have another review, and he'll tell me "much better!" But no. On each rewrite, I was disappointed. We'd talk again, and I'd try again. Over and over, until I was sure we were talking past each other. I was seeing the world one way and he was seeing it another way. I started to tell myself this whole book was all a big mistake. I was kidding myself that I could be a decent writer. Maybe I should just get a different coach and go back to my three-slide story.

> ***Testing*** *had started. Now I was mirroring Dave and Phil pre-senting their LTE solution to DSP companies in Chapter 3. I'd sort of got the right idea, the headline view, but I hadn't understood the full implications yet. I realized I didn't get it, and I was in trouble. I'd hit a serious setback, and I was wallowing in negative self-storytelling.*

We talked about this experience afterward—how I was struggling, feeling I'd made a mistake. David told me about his early teaching experience, in classes on creative writing.

"I found that it's not natural for people to give and get constructive criticism. It's a skill they have to learn. When we start to write, we all fall in love with our work. Somehow when your words are on a page, they have more meaning. Beginning writers are very sensitive about those words. They can't take criticism. You're calling their baby ugly. Over time, the more they work at it, they get used to killing their babies. But it takes guidance and time."

I recognized that weakness in myself. "You know," I told him, "I started out the same way. I'd hear a criticism and have this knee-jerk reaction. How dare you criticize my work? I've learned especially for written criticism, maybe it's best to leave it for a day or two. Or read it but then walk away. A day or two later, go back and read it again, with a more constructive mindset."

David laughed. "Yeah, the same with verbal criticism. You got it!"

He pointed me to a great TED talk[53] to help me snap out of my funk and get me thinking more constructively. I should stop obsessing over what I thought he was trying to tell me and think more about why my attempts at storytelling weren't working. I remembered particularly a couple of his hints, suggesting that I add dialogue and descriptive detail.

---

53   Jodie Rogers's "The stories we tell ourselves"– not coincidentally.

I found it easiest to start by adding dialogue. In Chapter 1, when it was my turn to present to Mitsubishi, I originally described what happened as a sequence of events: I presented to them without slides, they started to warm up, and we had a discussion around issues that hadn't been fixed, checking priorities. Now I turned those events into a dialogue, giving the characters voices. I don't remember the exact words (it was twenty years ago), but I remember the general sense—the meeting is burned into my memory. As I was building these dialogues, an amazing thing happened: I started to have fun. I remembered an additional physical detail here and there, like the heat in the room, the blue uniforms the Mitsubishi engineers wore, rolling up my sleeves—all of which added more color. Stories started to pop off the page. What I had always thought of as "nonessential background" made these stories much more engaging.

I had to work hard at descriptions. I remembered a few things, but I'm generally not so good at recalling "nonessential" details. I was lucky in Chapter 2 that John East remembered details of his meeting at Aerospace Corporation—the conference room, the table and seating, the general walking around the room catching up with everyone. David continued to nudge me; I looked back to John's description as an example, and started to recover little bits and pieces in my own stories. In Chapter 1, I remembered the long flights to Japan and the food. Really good, easy to recall. I remembered the framed prints in the Mitsubishi conference rooms. I prodded others for details—the back deck at Jim's house, the conference hall in Barcelona, the office in Calgary, the place Ajoy had breakfast with Mike. Small details to add a sense of place to the stories. Because to be involved, we have to imagine ourselves in a story, and that's a lot easier if we can imagine what's around us.

> *I'm still working on this skill—being observant, paying attention to what's around me and especially to the people around me. I try harder to remember names, something I have always found a struggle. Now I remember the names of people I meet, and they also remember me by name. Good practice for seeing others in the role of hero!*

Dialogue and descriptions helped a lot, but I was still missing something. David prodded some more, so I reread those sections and the feedback. I started to notice something strange about the pace of my writing. The story would be moving along at a reasonable tempo. I was having fun, watching the scene unfold, reliving the moment. Then suddenly I had to rush to the next milestone, as if I'd realized I was falling behind. No more dialogue or description. Not even more explanation. I had to close this paragraph—now!

I know where this comes from: my industry training. Every activity is governed by getting to the finish line, a decent finish, as quickly and efficiently as possible. Here I'd be enjoying myself, and then my conscience would pipe up, "Oh, no! Enough relaxing! I need to get to the next paragraph!" All that other detail, even explanations, jettisoned to meet a self-imposed deadline.

> *This may well be the first commandment of Silicon Valley. Obsessive focus on the goal. Anything else should be crushed.*

Fans of *The Big Bang Theory* will probably remember Amy's analysis of *Raiders of the Lost Ark*. If Indiana Jones (the hero) weren't in the movie, the Nazis would still have discovered the Ark of the Covenant, would still have taken it to the island, would still have opened it, and would still all have died. Logically, the storyline didn't need the hero at all. But without Indy, there would have been no rival at the outset, no love story, no clever idea to find the Ark, everything that drew us in. All that "nonessential" detail is essential to our emotional involvement in the story. The same applies to our stories, logic and efficiency be damned. We have to engage our audience emotionally: excitement, anticipation, even fear. A high-speed sprint to the finish kills the mood.

In our stories, we always want to race to the finish line—deal closed, investment signed, partnership agreed. I do it instinctively. It's hard to put aside years of training, to shed this habit of making the outcome vastly more important than anything else. But to tell a good story, to communicate with conviction, we must. The journey is just as important, worth recording and enjoying, especially in storytelling, because our audience will remember more of the details—people, surroundings, and dialogue. Details add depth and authenticity and make the story memorable. More importantly, people's imaginations are engaged, and they see themselves in your story. Our final goal is still important, but it's just another stop somewhere further along the road. No need to worry about that right now.

> I approached the **inner cave.**

Echoing Stephen King again, I didn't have all my stories figured out as I was writing this book. For Chapter 6, on marketing, I had no idea what the story would be. I assumed I'd think of something when I got there. I had plenty of raw material; I've been blogging for over five years. However, I didn't know how to make it dramatic. For each blog, I'd read a white paper, maybe have a call, then write the entry. How could I turn that into a story which could stand beside the Mars rover or automating cancer detection or contributing to supercomputing? Where would I find a dramatic arc, my Hero's Journey, all the stuff I need for a good story?

*The real **ordeals** started. In Greek mythology, the gods pun-*
ished Sisyphus by forcing him to push a boulder up a mountain.
Each time he neared the top, the boulder rolled back down, and
he had to start over. Over and over again. Chapter 6 became my
Sisyphean ordeal. Re-writing, over and over again.

My first pass was to admit defeat. There was no way to fashion a story out of all these blogs. Instead, I should write a how-to guide on creating blogs, positioning this chapter as a change of pace from the other stories, essentially reverting to my first instinct on the whole book. Maybe no one would notice? David noticed and gave that draft a big thumbs-down. He thought I could do better. I appreciated the vote of confidence, but I was rather more convinced I'd met my match.

I tried again. I would build a story around a very successful blog I'd written, one that got huge readership in one of the big industry magazines. I had ghostwritten that blog, so I needed permission to tell the story, and would have to write it in a way which preserved confidentiality. That draft took a while to develop but looked promising. I sent it to the client for review and approval. They turned me down flat; I could not publish that story. Now I was staring at a serious setback. Two attempts and I still had nothing but a hole where Chapter 6 should be. I was getting nervous, already approaching my publisher's first deadline. And I didn't have a clue what to do.

There's an important lesson here. I was trying to build a story
on something with a big finish. Where was the story? A good
story isn't defined by a big finish. It's defined by the whole jour-
ney.[54]

---

54   David sent me a Zen proverb: Obstacles do not block the path; they are the path.

Somewhere in the stream of advice David periodically sends me, he mentioned Jocko. Jocko is a retired Navy SEAL officer, an author who also hosts a podcast. A seriously type-A dude. One of his podcasts is called "GOOD." He tells a story about a subordinate coming to him with a major problem. Jocko tells him, "Good." Every time this guy comes to him with a problem, Jocko tells him, "Good." The guy finally asks why Jocko is always telling him "Good." Jocko replies that wherever there's a problem, something good can come from it if you approach it in the right way. Instead of obsessing about hitting a brick wall and the plan falling apart, there's an opportunity to rethink the problem, find a better solution, or take more time to prepare. Or even just to learn from the experience, to avoid the problem in the future.

I'm not a Jocko type, but I have to admit I liked this idea, so I put it to work on fixing my Chapter 6 problem. I told myself a story. I've been writing about storytelling for months and here's a setback. Wait—that's what happens in stories! What happens next? Well, let's look at it just as Jocko advises: this isn't a problem, it's an opportunity to grow. I had an opportunity to find a new solution, something even better than the last idea I had. Telling myself that story didn't solve the problem for me, but it completely changed my mindset. I was going to find a solution, and it was going to be even better than my last attempt. Once I believed I could do better, it didn't take long to find a better option. I chose a story about my journey in blogging. Not everything, but some of the highlights, more or less chronologically. My journey in becoming a better blogger. Again, David shot that down. What I'd written didn't have much to do with storytelling. It was all about writing technique. Wrong focus!

> *I was really starting to relate to Sisyphus. The guy got a raw deal. He was trying hard and kept on trying, motivating himself to find a way. Why couldn't he catch a break?*

And then a light dawned. My problem was that I was trying to build a complete Hero's Journey as my story, after telling you earlier in Chapter 6 that you can't fit a complete journey into the word count you have for a blog. Duh! If I wanted to show you how blogs work, I had to follow my own advice. Not tell a single story, but a series of short stories illustrating a number of types of blog. With that breakthrough, I rewrote Chapter 6 for the fourth time. With fingers crossed, I handed it back to David. He liked it! Finally, I could stop rolling that danged rock up the hill!

> *This is a reminder that the Hero's Journey isn't a straitjacket. It's a very good guide in most cases, but when it doesn't work, go with what makes the most sense, as long as you're telling exciting stories. At last, I was on the **road back**.*

Since by now you know the Hero's Journey, you know my journey isn't really over. I still have to face a final challenge. A challenge which will lead to a resurrection. That challenge was this final chapter, the stories we tell ourselves. I thought, "OK, so we talk to ourselves. We all do. What does that have to do with storytelling?" David and I had another conversation.

He said, "Go back to that critical customer meeting, the date you're going on tonight, the tough meeting with an employee, forgetting your spouse's birthday. You could read any one of a million books that would tell you how to prepare. Maybe you'd learn something. Maybe it would help you survive that upcoming experience that made you so anxious. Until the next time, when you'd be back at square one. As if you learned to perform a trick one time. Because you don't use it all the time, it didn't stick as a life skill."

David told me about work he's done with a PGA professional who talks about the difference between pros and amateurs, a difference that is much more psychological than physical.[55] As I see it, pros replace one big crushing goal, like winning the game, with a journey through a lot of smaller goals. Enjoying the walk down each fairway, the view of the lake, breathing well, aiming to reduce their number of putts for the round. Some goals not even directly related to the game. A journey through multiple subgoals in which they'll experience enjoyment, some successes, some setbacks. They'll learn how they might improve elements of the next journey—a journey they don't measure as pass/fail, but by the sum of measures on each step.

What he said next grabbed my attention. Simply having a planned journey isn't enough. Pros have to make sure they stick to the plan. Before they start a game, they put themselves into a *flow state*, a state in which their only important objective is to follow that journey. They block distractions and upsets. Maybe that last drive wasn't so good, but that's not important now. They've moved on to thinking about the next step in their journey.

I chewed on this for a little while, then said, "That flow state point is really interesting. I get it, but for me it prompted a slightly different view, a reinterpretation that snaps the journeys in this book into focus. I finally understand *why* I was able to make my Mitsubishi meeting a success. Yes, I went through all the steps in the journey. I made them the hero of the story, I told them about everything we had done for them. All that stuff. But I didn't know I was on a journey. What propelled me along that path?

---

55   Equally true in many other fields.

"I finally get it. I followed that path because I was backed into a corner. My flow was driven by desperation—a desperate need to regain trust. Sticking to my original path wouldn't get me there. I had to take some other path. Desperation drove me to describe what we *had* achieved. To emphasize the best story I could: our commitment to the needs of our hero, our journey toward delivering what they wanted. Which ultimately was a much better story than my slides. Not an ending to a story, a status update, but the journey to find an ending. Desperation kept me focused on the journey, focused on the hero's needs, ready to deal with interruptions and digressions along the way. Ready to welcome digressions as evidence that I might be breaking through."

Now I understand that the journey is the goal; it must be the center of our attention. The destination will take care of itself. This mindset doesn't come naturally. PGA pros hypnotize or meditate themselves into this state. In business and in life, we can find other ways to put the journey first. My desperate need to regain trust drove me along that path at Mitsubishi, as it did for John in the Mars rover story and Peter in the Cray story. Jim was motivated by a passion to honor his wife's memory after losing her to cancer; he obsessively checked each step, avoiding Theranos shortcuts. Dave and Phil were motivated by another compelling need—to find their story and create something important. In my blogging, I was motivated by an obsession to improve, in my writing and in storytelling. Ajoy was motivated by his investors' desire to see their investment bear fruit. In this last chapter, I have again been compelled by an obsession, this time to write the best possible book that I can, despite constant setbacks. In each case, the goal was the journey: regaining trust, guiding a venture, finding a story, searching for an exit, becoming a better writer.

*The **resurrection**. The Hero's Journey gave me the map. I also needed single-minded determination to stay on the journey—a "damn the torpedoes" commitment that would drive me along the journey no matter what my weaker instincts might suggest. The kind of commitment required to reach for real progress.*

I consider myself a hardheaded pragmatist, not much given to speculation on Eastern philosophies, but I have come to accept that the journey is more important than the destination. I always knew in a general sense that it is important to enjoy the life we are living, not the life we hope to live when we get to some dreamed-of destination. Now I realize this is equally true in storytelling, even in business. We have business goals to meet, but we don't have to rush to meet those goals. It is much more important to find the right path to the right goal. And to make sure that we keep ourselves on the journey. Telling ourselves stories can help us find that path.

*I **returned with the elixir**. I now understood the importance of the journey and of sticking to it, enjoying small successes along the way, finding a way through setbacks, accepting help from mentors and allies to keep my spirits up—to tell me a more positive story when I couldn't find such a story myself, when I felt I couldn't continue. Always staying the course.*

This reminds me of Frodo's journey from the Shire to Mount Doom. It was a long journey filled with many challenges. Sometimes Frodo needed to lean on encouragement from Gandalf, sometimes from Sam, but he was always pressing forward. Sticking to the journey.

TAKEAWAYS

We define our success or failure at each step of our lives through the stories we tell ourselves. We usually don't put a lot of thought into those stories. We know the beginning, we know the ending we'd like to see, or maybe the ending we dread. We march through what seem to us logical steps from beginning to end. What else can we do?

But life, both business and personal, is not an engineering problem with a clear, logical path leading without fail to the best solution. Our partners, friends, clients, and colleagues, even our adversaries, are heroes with their own goals in life. Each of us cycles through our own motivations, journeys, and schedules, remaining in comfortable stasis, resisting change, until we are challenged or forced to jump into an adventure promising great accomplishment but fraught with risk.

Great things happen when heroes and their mentors embrace that risk and set out on the journey. The most important of these happen along the journey, not at the end—when the hero and mentor find each other and recognize the opportunity; when they commit to a new and challenging path; in facing tests, learning from failures, building skills, and gathering allies; in the ordeal, the major challenge, where mentor and hero both prove their worth and develop a trust in each other that can only come from overcoming that trial together. We all dream of the resurrection and elixir, but dreams don't deliver accomplishments. It's the journey that gets us there, with a determined intent not to cut corners, to dig into and complete every step as well as we possibly can.

Appreciate the journey and your companions. Though you may struggle at times, you're learning how to empathize with your audience, customer, employee, partner, or friend. Show that you respect them and want to take the time to understand their needs. They in turn will be encouraged to respect you and your needs. You'll gain a mutual understanding through the journey which will lead to better outcomes and a wider circle of heroes, allies, and mentors who can support you in future adventures.

CODA

I've been telling you stories about myself and others, but you are the real hero of this book. My intention has been to serve as your mentor, to help you realize your vision and full potential. I want my stories to spark your imagination, to help you build and tell a story that will raise your audience to hero status, pull them to the edge of their seats, make them see you as a wise and experienced mentor who can help them reach for greatness, leave them buzzing with excitement after your talk, now imagining how they might build on your story to help them accelerate their own.

Find your stories. Now that you know how to tell them, they're a lot more interesting than you ever imagined. Your audience will thank you, and your business will prosper—not on every telling, but more often than the low hit rate you may have resigned yourself to.

If you have a story you want to share, please feel free to post to **tale@findthestory.net**. I'll enjoy your stories, and I'll provide feedback as time permits. Perhaps if this book proves popular, I may plan a sequel, building on some of your stories. Either way, I consider my journey a success. I grew as a writer and, I believe, as a person. I hope you will find the same success!

ACKNOWLEDGMENTS

There are many people who contributed in one way or another to this book: through short and long stories, through background, through expert assistance, and through help and encouragement.

For stories, I'd like to thank particularly Brian Ascher of Venrock; Ajoy Bose, Chairman, President, and CEO of Atrenta; Peter Calverley, Chairman and for a while Acting CEO of CoolIT; Bert Clement, CEO of Retail Solutions; Lou Covey, an independent content marketing expert and principal in Footwasher Media; John East, now an angel investor and past CEO of Actel (now a part of Microchip); Jim Hogan, variously an angel investor and board member in many ventures; Dave Kelf, a marketing exec/business development advisor/consultant who has played a major role in multiple company repositionings and exits; and Dave Millman, heading BizDev.Global, advising early tech ventures across a broad spectrum.

For a lot of thought-provoking background and in some cases guidance through my earlier career, I'd like to thank: Ron Craig, now at Oracle and previously advising at Google and other SaaS providers; Mike Gianfagna, previously VP Marketing at eSilicon; John Rochfort, a seasoned expert in software sales; Sally Slemons, previously marketing communications at eSilicon and an expert in communications through digital media; and Jason Zeiler, product marketing at CoolIT and also an expert in social media communications.

A big thank-you to David Allen of Forbes and XLPO Ventures for pushing me to become a better writer. This book would be nowhere near where it is now without his help.

Another big thank-you to Judy, Mary, and Holly Kane for putting up with me and endlessly entertaining me on my frequent trips to San Jose.

And finally, a huge thank you to my wife, Laura, for humoring me and supporting me in this project. Maybe she'll see more of me now this project is done!